TABLE OF CONTENTS

INTRODUCTION

News about reductions in military spending and the impact of sequestration have dominated recent headlines. Both civil and military leaders have expressed deep-seated concerns about the impact of defense cuts imposed by sequestration to national security. This paper seeks to provide some context by looking at previous reductions in defense spending. Historically the U.S. has followed a pattern of significant defense cuts following the conclusion of conflicts in search of a peace dividend which allows the country to focus more on domestic issues, and today is no different. Figure 1 (pg.5) illustrates this point.

U.S. defense spending is cyclical in nature meaning there is no one factor that determines the size and nature of the defense budget. The international security environment, employment of forces conducting war, and domestic economic and political sentiments of the American people are major factors that have determined the country's path regarding to strategy and resources.

There is no denying the pressure to scale back on defense spending as the U.S. winds down from over a decade of war. Today, the challenging fiscal and economic situation provides a looming backdrop for significant debate on future levels of U.S. defense spending. This time the question is: What kind of affordable defense budget is needed in order to ensure preparedness for the challenges of the uncertain years ahead? This is a question America has faced since the beginning of the Cold War. The challenge is not new, but current economic, political, and strategic conditions are new. The purpose of this thesis is to illustrate through case study analysis relevant historical insights from past post-war military drawdowns that should be applied to current budget decisions in

1

order not to end up with a "hollow force" incapable of executing the National Security Strategy.

Origins of the Hollow Force

This definition and historical synopsis of "hollow force" is here to provide context for the consumer of this research:

> A hollow force is one in which unit effectiveness is systemically degraded, resulting in authorized US forces presenting the illusion of readiness. Deficiencies in resourcing for training, unit equipment, or operations and maintenance could hollow out the force. Similarly, system-wide problems with morale and retention could hamper aggregate unit effectiveness. Likewise, high levels of readiness for unplanned contingencies can come at the expense of operational planning preparedness, and vice versa.[1]

Recent news headlines about reductions in military spending and impact of sequestration have many political and military leaders concerned that the reductions in defense spending could lead to a hollow force. Warnings from political and military leaders of a hollow force evoke memories of periods following World War II, Korea, Vietnam, and the post-Cold War period of the 1990s. The two periods in history that are commonly used to characterize the state of the U. S. military as a hollow force was the U.S. military post-Vietnam and the post-Cold War 90s.[2] The gravest concern in the post-Vietnam force was the quality of personnel. It was widely perceived that the U.S. military conventional warfighting capabilities that had declined as the Vietnam War came to a close did not appear to be recovering adequately, particularly as the military services struggled to adapt to the All-Volunteer Force.[3]

---

[1] CSAF Strategic Studies Group, *What is a Hollow Force?* http://www.af.mil/shared/media/document/AFD-120213-053.pdf (assessed December 15, 2012).

[2] Andrew Feickert, and Stephen Daggett. *A Historical Perspective on Hollow Forces,* Washington, D.C: Congressional Research Service, 2012, 10. <http://www.fas.org/sgp/crs/natsec/R42334.pdf>.(accessed Feb 10, 2013).

[3] Ibid., 14

In the early 1990s after the Cold War, the U.S military was regarded as highly capable, but there was concern that the steep defense budget cuts being implemented would rapidly erode the gains made in attaining quality personnel, and the growing commitments to contingency operations abroad also put a strain on personnel and disrupted preparations for major conflicts as recruitment and retention concerns began to emerge.[4]

Defining the current Problem

Following a lengthy debate over raising the debt limit, the Budget Control Act (BCA) of 2011 was signed into law by President Obama on August 2, 2011. The Budget Control Act imposed a series of measures to limit spending and decrease the nation's debt. In an effort to facilitate where the budget reductions would come from, the law created a Joint Select Committee (referred to as the "Super Committee" made up of members from the U.S. House of Representative and the U.S. Senate, Democrats and Republicans) on Deficit Reductions to identify $1.5 trillion in deficit reduction over the period of fiscal years (FYs) 2012-2021. The Joint Committee was simply charged with achieving deficit reductions without restrictions on how to accomplish the net reductions in the deficit. The law also created a fail-safe mechanism called sequestration if the Super Committee failed to identify these savings, or Congress failed to approve the Super Committee's recommendation. A series of automatic cuts would go into effect, affecting every federal program not specifically excluded on January 1, 2013. The Super Committee failed, and sequestration was set to go into effect at the close of 2012.

As the terms of the BCA drew closer, U.S. policy makers found themselves in a policy conundrum of unintended consequences, which became known as the "fiscal

---

[4] Ibid., 14

cliff." The fiscal cliff would have increased taxes by ending the temporary payroll tax cuts and rolled back the Bush era tax cuts. On top of the tax increases, the BCA enacted spending cuts which totaled $1.2 trillion over ten years would have gone into effect. According to an article written by Jim McTague for Barron's, a respected financial periodical, over 1,000 government programs--including the defense budget-- were in line for deep automatic cuts. The tax increases, which were seen as the larger burdens on the economy, prompted congressional action.[5] A part of the "fiscal cliff" deal was to delay sequestration until March 1, 2013 giving policy makers more time to consider possible budget reduction compromises and defense leaders more time to consider possible courses of action in the event sequestration went into effect.

Military budget cuts are nothing new to the United States and the military has historically taken its fair share of budget cuts. As the drawdown in defense spending continues, the ability of the Department Defense (DoD) to maintain the readiness of its military forces is the subject of growing debate. DoD has already been impacted by the $487 billion over 10 years as required by the Budget Control Act of 2011, and now DoD is set to absorb an additional 10 percent cut over the next ten years should political leaders fail to agree on an alternative to the sequestration cuts.[6] In the midst of sequestration, it has become apparent to military leaders the challenges the Services face in adequately supporting the goals and objectives of the National Security Strategy.

Objective and Scope

---

[5] Jim McTague, "Steering Clear of the Cliff," *Barron's*. http://online.barrons.com/article/SB50001424053111904706204578004182169208520.html (accessed Feb 10, 2013).
[6] Clark A Murdoch, Planning for a Deep Defense Drawdown--part I, *Center for Strategic & International Studies*, May 2012. www.csis.org/files/publication/120522_DD_Interim_Report.pdf (assessed Febuary 23, 2013).

The United States has routinely drawn down forces following the completion of major conflicts in search of a peace dividend; however, defense leaders have invoked the specter of a hollow force to describe what can happen if the U.S. repeat the mistakes of past defense drawdowns. Part of this thesis analysis will entail evaluating four-post conflict periods and their defense strategies to glean lessons applicable to the current period of reductions.

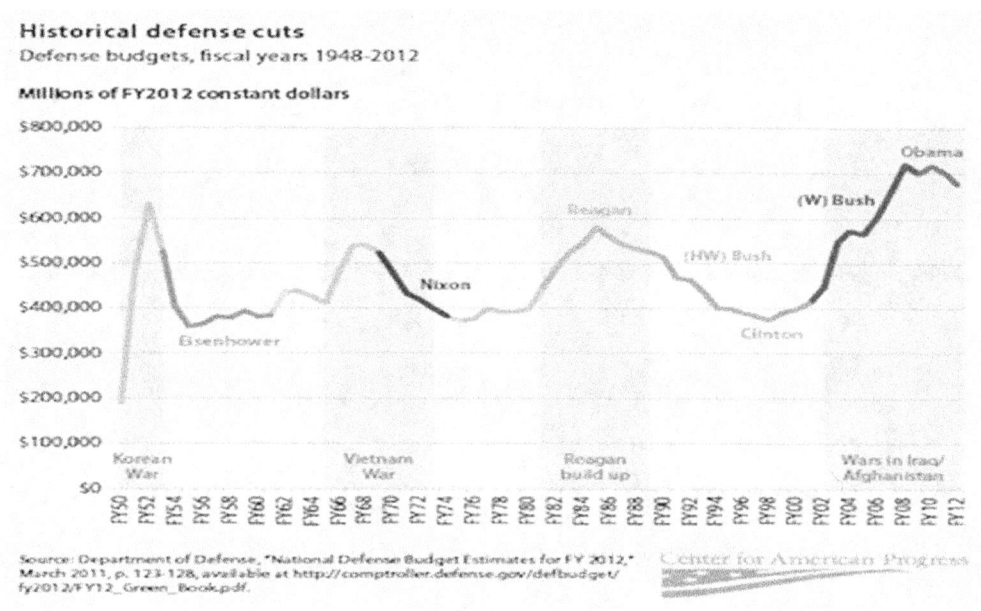

Figure 1. Historical Defense Cuts[7]

---

[7] Lawrence J. Korb, Laura Conley, and Alex Rothman. "A Return to Responsibility," *Center for American Progress*, July 14, 2011, www.americanprogress.org/issues/security (assessed January 15, 2013).

CHAPTER 2: FRAMING THE ISSUE

Overview

This chapter reviews the cyclic history of United States defense spending and sets the stage for a closer examination of past military drawdowns. It begins with an acknowledgement of the fundamental competition between economic and military power and a graphic history of the United States' periodic defense mobilization and demobilization. The drawdowns are shown to be driven by both fiscal constraints and strategic philosophy. This dilemma is not new. A number of presidents from both parties have faced similar circumstances since the end of World War II.

A brief case analysis on defense sizing introduces different strategic perspectives on the proper level of peacetime military forces. This chapter will provide the framework for detailed analysis of the current fiscal environment facing President Obama and Congress as they determine how much to spend on defense as the nation approaches the final years of the Afghanistan war and faces large budget deficits, debt, and an uncertain future threat environment.

Post World War II Strategy and Policy Conundrum

Initially the Army and Navy had separately determined during the war their reasonable postwar strengths and had produced plans for an orderly demobilization. Demobilization plans called for release of troops on an individual basis and were aimed at producing a systematic peacetime military structure. The Navy developed a program for 600,000 men, and 370 combat and 5,000 other ships, and 8,000 aircraft. The Army Air Forces was equally specific, setting its sights on becoming a separate service with 400,000 members, 70 combat groups, and a complete organization of supporting units.

The Army initially established as an overall postwar goal a regular and reserve structure capable of mobilizing 4 million men within a year of any future outbreak of war; later it set the strength of active ground and air forces at 1.5 million.[1]

The World War II drawdown was primarily focused on demobilizing a nation at war and reconverting the use of American industries, natural resources and labor force to a sustainable peacetime economy. There were competing interests between the troops and military leaders. Millions of draftees remained overseas due to the rapid end of the war. The troops that remained abroad began demanding discharges because many of them remembered the Depression years and the large-scale unemployment. They wanted to get out of uniform and back to civilian life. Military leaders were in no hurry to demobilize for wanting to keep large forces under arms in order to retain large budgets.[2] Congress ordered the services to get moving on demobilization and get troops mustered out and back to work in civilian jobs[3]

President Truman's top concerns as the nation emerged from World War II were on prevent an economic downturn, address the nation's finances and public debt, provide for social programs, and build a durable economy.[4] He found himself at odds with the civilian and uniformed leaders in the Pentagon, whose request for more money he felt would have put new burdens on the budget at the very time when his priority was to check inflation by cutting spending and reducing the war-swollen national debt.[5] Truman wanted the armed forces sufficiently strong enough to signal American resolve in the face

---

[1] Richard W. Stewart, American Military History, Volume II: *The United States Army in a Global Era, 1917-2008*. Washington, D.C. (Center of Military History, 2010), 77.

[2] Forrest Pogue and Drew Middleton, *George C. Marshall Statesman, 1945-1959*. New York: Viking Penguin, 1987, 55.

[3] Robert J. Donovan, *Tumultuous Years: The Presidency of Harry S. Truman, 1949-1953*. (New York: Norton, 1982), 516.

[4] Ibid., 520.

[5] Ibid., 540.

of Soviet truculence in Europe. He saw no need for an increase in military spending, largely because he did not anticipate another war.[6]

Truman saw America's atomic monopoly as a valuable asset in achieving lasting peace; and from a foreign policy perspective, he believed America's atomic monopoly was a key diplomatic tool in advancing US interests in the world. Most American officials, and even the majority of scientists in the United States, believed that it would be many years before the Soviets could develop an atomic bomb of their own, and by that time the United States would have achieved a vast numeric superiority. He did not want to sacrifice a balanced budget for military expenditures that he believed could not guarantee national security.

The Truman Doctrine was an admission that Truman's approach was flawed. The broad parameters of U.S. Cold War foreign policy required containment of the Soviet Union and the United States taking on the commitment to provide military and economic assistance to protect nations from communist aggression.

In September 1949, the Soviets exploded a nuclear device, ending the U.S. monopoly and creating a new level of strategic uncertainty. He reacted by requesting an intensive re-evaluation of America's strategic situation by the National Security Council. The report, issued to the president in early 1950, called for massive increases in military spending and a dramatic acceleration in the program to develop the next stage of nuclear weaponry—the hydrogen bomb. The President was alarmed at Soviet expansion into clearly strategic areas of the world--even those countries arguably beyond America's sphere of influence, namely Iran, Turkey and Greece. He saw Soviet pressures on Iran

---

[6] Melvyn P. Leffler, *A Preponderance of Power: National Security, the Truman Administration, and the Cold War*. Stanford, Calif: Stanford University Press, 1992.

and Turkey as an immediate threat to the global balance of power. President Truman began to pursue a much stronger military policy, along with his economic or political policies, to contain the Soviets.[7] Under NSC-68[8] he asked for increased military spending to $45-50 billion a year in 1950, which was more than three times the $13,000,000,000 appropriation for 1950. The main aim of those funds was to build the North Atlantic Treaty Organization (NATO) military structure in Europe .[9] The perceived threat by the Soviets led Truman to pursue this strategy which he rightly considered essential. After 1949, the Truman administration became more concerned with maintaining a balance of power than fiscal pressures on the budget. President Truman went on to warn Congress that "we must guard against the folly of attempting budget slashes which would impair our prospects for peace or cripple the programs essential to our national strength.[10]

Truman's unexpected conflict

The FY 1950 defense spending remained flat and DoD to-date had reduced its military manpower by 88 percent following World War II, reaching a low of 1.5 million.[11] Manpower reductions were followed by decreases in funding for the Army and Navy, while DoD increased emphasis on research, development and acquisition, largely for the Air Force to deliver nuclear weapons. Military manpower then or today, was

---

[7] Robert J. Donovan, 146

[8] National Security Council Paper 68 which is frequently referred to as NSC-68 was a Top-Secret report issued by the United States National Security Council on April 14, 1950, during the presidency of Harry S. Truman. It was one of the most significant document of American policy in the Cold War. NSC-68 largely shaped U.S. foreign policy in the Cold War and involved a decision to make Containment against Communist expansion a high priority.

[9] Robert J. Donovan, 158

[10] J. Woolley, and G. Peters, *Harry S. Truman: Annual Message to the Congress on the State of the Union,*" January 4, 1950. The American Presidency Project. http://www.presidency.ucsb.edu/ws/index.php?pid=13567#izz1krXZK4H4 (accessed Febuary 18, 2013).

[11] U.S. Department of Defense. *Department of Defense Budget Estimates 2012.* http://comptroller.defense.gov/defbudget/fy2013/budget_justification/index.html, 95(accessed Febuary 18, 2013).

DoD's primary cost driver in FY 1950, consuming 47 percent of the defense budget.[12] The other significant expenses were operations and maintenance. In FY 1950, DoD allocated its resources uniformly between the services (Air Force $16.5 billion, 33 percent; Army $16 billion, 32 percent; and Navy/Marine Corp $16 billion, 32 percent) while reserving $3 billion for Defense-Wide activities (2 percent).[13] DoD failed to match resources to strategy in its FY 1950 budget. There was no priority of allocation meet primary mission areas.

On June 25, 1950, the attack by the North Korean People's Army against the Republic of Korea caught President Truman and the nation off guard. The term "Hollow Force" first entered the lexicon in 1950 at the outset of the Korean War when the U.S. found itself woefully unprepared for a conflict in Asia. The poor performance of Army ground forces was blamed on the rapid draw-down of forces after World War II, which crippled peacetime. The task force lacked the proper equipment and training to carry out the mission it was assigned. A North Korean tank column overran the task force and continued its advance south eventually overwhelming American positions forcing the Americans to retreat.[14]

After the failures of Task Force Smith, a U.S. task force of 400 infantry and one artillery battery which was woefully unprepared to delay advancing North Korean forces until additional U.S. troops arrived in the country to form a stronger defensive line. Opinions vary on the real cause of failure; however, the facts remain that the Army of

---

[12] U.S. Department of Defense. *Department of Defense Budget Estimates2012*. http://comptroller.defense.gov/defbudget/fy2013/budget_justification/index.html, 95 (accessed Febuary 18, 2013).

[13] Ibid.

[14] J. Lawton Collins, *War in Peacetime; The History and Lessons of Korea*, (Boston: Houghton Mifflin, 1969), 45.

1950 was short of personnel and relied heavily on World War II equipment that was often worn out and lacked spare parts. [15]

After initial success under General Douglas MacArthur in September 1950, the intervention of Chinese Communist Forces led to a three-year long brutal and bloody stalemate that finally ended in an armistice, freezing the conflict to this day. The cost of the war was significant 55,000 Americans were killed. The Korean War buildup forced the nation to triple its defense spending from $192 billion in 1950 to $606 billion per year through 1952. [16] DoD doubled its active military manpower from 1.5 million to 3.6 million during this time. The Army grew from 593,000 to 1.6 million; the Marine Corps grew from 74, 000 to 249,000. [17] DoD also made significant increases in procurement, increasing from $37 billion to $235 billion between 1950 and 1952. [18]

New Look

Throughout his eight years as president, Eisenhower based his New Look national security policy upon the conception of the Cold War struggle that he had formulated in the late 1940s. His waging of the Cold War would not include provocative operations to destabilize the Soviet Union and its allied regimes in Eastern Europe. Instead, he still envisaged the Cold War as a long term trial, one that the American people and economy had to be prepared to wage indefinitely. In this struggle between two competing ideological systems, Eisenhower sincerely believed that the incredible defense build-up outlined originally in the Truman administration's NSC 68 in 1950 could not be sustained

---

[15] Ibid., 47.
[16] Gerhard Peters and John T. Woolley, "Harry S. Truman, Annual Budget Message to the Congress: Fiscal Year 1950," The American Presidency Project, (assessed January 15, 2013). http://www.presidency.ucsb.edu/ws/?pid=13434
[17] Ibid.
[18] Ibid.

without eventually subverting the principles of a free-market economy, thus transforming the country into a "garrison state." Since significant reductions in domestic government operations were not politically feasible, the only alternative was a new, more economical defense posture.[19] Eisenhower strove to ensure the defense budget was dictated by national strategy and not politics.

The Opportunity Cost of Defense Spending

President Eisenhower's defense policy was guided by his recognition that there is an opportunity cost to defense spending. That is, money spent on defense diverts resources from other investments that can support the long-term prosperity of the American people. President Eisenhower slashed defense spending by 27 percent during his eight years in office. He took office in 1953 in the midst of the Korean War, where he inherited a wartime budget of $526 billion dollars; and by the time he left office in 1961, defense spending had been reduced to $382 billion. Eisenhower achieved these reductions by drawing down spending on military personnel, operations and maintenance, and procurement. At the same time, he increased funding for research, development, test, and evaluation (RDT&E). He invested in the technologies that would prepare the American military for the future and maintain a technological edge over the Soviet Union.[20]

Like President Truman, President Eisenhower believed U.S. security was tied to the health of the economy. In keeping with this belief, he strategically cut defense spending from wartime peaks in order to free up resources for critical investments in the

---

[19] John Lewis Gaddis, *Cold War Statesmen Confront the Bomb: Nuclear Diplomacy Since 1945,* (New York: Oxford University Press, 1999), 67.

[20] Scott Horton, Eisenhower on the Opportunity Cost of Defense. The Stream. http://harpers.org/blog/2007/11/eisenhower-on-the-opportunity-cost-of-defense-spending/ (accessed January/10, 2013).

U.S. military and economy while balancing the budget. President Eisenhower reduced service budgets substantially and cut over a million service members from wartime highs after the end of the Korean War in July 1953 into a more fiscally sustainable force that coincided with his national defense strategy. Eisenhower's faith in deterrence reinforced his belief that the United States could use force in localized crises without fearing escalation to general war. However, the nuclear forces of the Navy and Air Force were reduced by much smaller amounts. The majority of defense cuts came from the aquisition budget, which was reduced by $83 billion, or 49 percent.[21]

Intervention in Indochina

Like Truman, Eisenhower provided military aid to the French, who had begun fighting a war in 1946 to regain control over their colonial possession of Indochina, which included the current nations of Cambodia, Laos, and Vietnam. By 1954, the Eisenhower administration was paying more than 75 percent of the French costs of the war. Yet the French were unable to defeat the Vietminh, a nationalist force under the leadership of the Communist Ho Chi Minh.

On August 4, 1953, President Eisenhower spoke before the U.S. Governors' Conference and warned that the political and military situation in Asia had become very ominous for the U.S. He defended his decision to approve a $400 million aid package to help the French in their effort as "the cheapest way that we can prevent the occurrence that would be of most terrible significance to the United States."[22] He cited the need to defend French-run Indochina as the French military battled communist Vietnamese

---

[21] John Lewis Gaddis, *Cold War Statesmen Confront the Bomb: Nuclear Diplomacy Since 1945*, (New York: Oxford University Press, 1999,) 135.

[22] Mount Holyoke College, "President Eisenhower's Remarks at Governors' Conference," https://www.mtholyoke.edu/acad/intrel/pentagon/ps7.htm (assessed June 9, 2013

revolutionaries for control of the country. President Eisenhower's speech invoked what became known as the "domino theory"--the notion a communist takeover in Indochina would lead other Asian nations to follow suit.[23] President Eisenhower was wary of getting the United States involved in a land war in Asia and he understood the political and escalation risk which is why he sent U.S. weapons and dollars instead.

Eisenhower hoped to salvage a partial victory by preventing Ho Chi Minh from establishing a Communist government over all of Vietnam. In 1954-1955, U.S. aid and support helped Ngo Dinh Diem establish a non-Communist government in South Vietnam. Eisenhower considered the creation of South Vietnam a significant Cold War success, yet his decision to commit U.S. prestige and power in South Vietnam created long-term dangers that his successors would have to confront.

Flexible Response

During the 1960 presidential campaign, Democrats charged that U.S. defense spending was inadequate, despite the fact that defense spending levels in 1960 accounted for nearly one-half of the budget and almost 10 percent of GNP. John F. Kennedy pledged to increase funding for a broad range of forces. At the start of his administration defense increases were modest and short-lived, as competing domestic program needs soon emerged.[24]

President Kennedy's initial budget program called for defense budget increases to support his new "flexible response" doctrine. Flexible Response was also a deterrent strategy like Eisenhower's New Look; but the difference was it entailed a capability to react across the entire spectrum of possible challenges, coping with anything from

---

[23] Ibid.
[24] Gaddis, 250.

9

general atomic war to infiltrations and aggressions such as what was occurring in Indo-China.[25]

Kennedy set out the objectives of this strategy in his first message to Congress in March 1961. Kennedy's strategic approach centered on five major areas: bolstering of conventional and unconventional military capabilities; strategic missile build-up; renewed efforts to solidify alliances; a new emphasis on the non-military instruments of containment and more effective management of domestic resources vital to defense. January 1962, President Kennedy formalized his national defense strategy, which was to provide a survivable strategic offensive force and a command and control system; an improved anti-bomber defense system and a civil defense program.

The crises over Berlin in 1961 and Cuba in 1962 added to President Kennedy's urgency for expanding defense. Three months after the Cuban missile crisis, the president submitted his budget to Congress announcing that there is no discount price for defense.[26] After Kennedy's assassination, the basic assumption of a "flexible response"-- having the capability to respond to aggression across the spectrum of warfare-- remained in place under Lyndon B. Johnson.

Vietnam and Defense Policy

After his 1964 presidential landslide victory, President Lyndon B. Johnson planned to implement the most ambitious domestic agenda since the New Deal. Johnson submitted his 1965 budget cutting defense by $800 million and shifting most of the funding to domestic programs. Johnson felt previous defense spending levels had

---

[25] B. Slantchev, *National Security Strategy: The Vietnam War, 1954-1975.* University of California-San Diego: University of California-San Diego, 2009, 55.

[26] Dennis S. Ippolito, *Blunting the Sword: Budget Policy and the Future of Defense.*(Washington, DC, National Defense University, 1994), 12

provided an advantage for the United States creating a more formidable defense establishment that was vastly superior to the Soviet nuclear force.[27] Defense spending in 1965 dropped by $4 billion, which was more than President Johnson had anticipated. This drop was the lowest since the Korean War buildup.[28]

As the U.S involvement in Vietnam deepened, defense spending began rising sharply; Johnson, however, resisted offsetting defense spending increases with cuts in domestic programs. Domestic spending was allowed to rise along with wartime defense spending. Major tax increases were repeatedly postponed.[29] The Johnson administration's refusal to subordinate its domestic policy agenda for increases in the defense budget ignited highly partisan and ideological differences over defense policy and budget. In 1968 Senate Armed Services Committee chairman Richard B. Russell announced that "we cannot continue to support a war, be capable of honoring our commitments abroad, and maintain an adequate defense posture without substantially increasing the size of our defense budget in the near future." [30] However, the political and public support for increases in defense spending waned as the opposition to the war began to take shape. Congress stopped pressing for more weapons systems and balanced forces as it had during the early stages of the Vietnam War.

While Johnson wanted to continue New Deal programs and expand welfare with his own Great Society programs, he was also in the arms race of the Cold War, and Vietnam War. Large defense and domestic programs put strains on the economy and Johnson felt the large defense budget hampered his Great Society programs.

---

[27] Dennis S. Ippolito, *Blunting the Sword: Budget Policy and the Future of Defense.* (Washington, DC, National Defense University, 1994), 31.
[28] Ibid, 32.
[29] Ibid, 32.
[30] Ibid, 35.

Post-Vietnam Downsizing

Defense spending during Vietnam reached its peak in FY 1967, and despite continuing increases in intensity of combat operations in Vietnam, DoD began implementing reductions by FY 1969.[31] The post-Vietnam drawdown basically began while troops were still engaged in combat.

This realistic constraint on the U.S. worldwide conventional capabilities was a major factor in reassessing defense strategy.[32] After Nixon was elected in 1968, he cut defense spending by more than $152 billion as he continued to reduce forces in Vietnam. President Nixon redirected wartime funding toward establishing new domestic programs as the post-Vietnam political environment and the public demanded a peace dividend. President Nixon's national military strategy was a shift from previous strategies founded on the U.S. military having the ability to fight two and a half wars simultaneously to a one and a half war strategy.[33] This change set the stage for dramatic personnel cuts. Between 1969 and 1972, the Army's active components was cut from 1.5 million to 780, 000 a 50 percent reduction.[34] In 1970, Congress cut defense spending, and continued that course through the seventies. Congress continued to pressure the Defense Department to reduce the size of the force. A reduction in force (RIF) was implemented in 1970 to rid the services of excess personnel accumulated during Vietnam. The RIF disproportionately affected reserve officers resulting in a great deal of turbulence and

---

[31] L.R. Jones and J. McCaffery, *Budgeting, Financial Management, and Acquisition Reform in the U.S. Department of Defens,*(Charlotte, N.C.: IAP-Information Age Pub., 2008), 8.
[32] Ibid, 8.
[33] David McCormick, *The Downsized Warrior: America's Army in Transition,* (New York: New York University Press, 1998), 57.
[34] John F.Shortal, "20th-Century Demobilization Lessons," *Military Review.* 78, no. 5: 1998, 64.

diminished morale throughout the ranks. The RIF forced seasoned combat veterans and junior officers from the ranks without warning.

President Nixon also campaigned on ending the draft and move toward an all-volunteer force. In 1973 President Nixon ended the draft, while acknowledging the fact that an all-volunteer force would cost more than a conscript force. The Total Force Policy allowed DoD to shrink the size of the active-duty armed forces while claiming that it did not. The Total Force concept had shifted nearly 70 percent of the active Army's combat service support to the reserves.[35] The Army became increasingly more senior in the upper ranks as its active and reserve post-Vietnam force began to take shape.[36]

The all-volunteer force resulted in a significant rise in manpower costs and criticisms of the all-volunteer concept involved focused on this very point. Compensation was certainly much higher than when 40 percent of the force was low-paid conscripts. Recruiting an all-volunteer force after Vietnam proved more difficult than some expected. DoD increased enlisted compensation by up to 76 percent resulting in a greater percentage of the budget being spent on manpower.[37] The all-volunteer force creates professionals with a higher proportion of married soldiers. Dependent-related expenses were added to total personnel costs. In addition to pay and benefits for all soldiers, the enlistment bonuses and educational entitlements needed to fill the ranks

---

[35] L.J. Korb, L. Conley, & A.A. Rothman , *A Return to Responsibility,* www.americanprogress.org/wp-content/.../07/.../defense_budgets.pdf (assessed April 25, 2013).
[36] Andrew Feickert and Charles A. Henning, Army Drawdown and Restructuring Background and Issues for Congress, *Congressional Research Service*, 2012. <http://www.fas.org/sgp/crs/natsec/R42493.pdf>.
[37] Bernard I. Rostker, *I Want You! The Evolution of the All-Volunteer Force,* (Santa Monica, CA: RAND, 2006), 345.

grew. Finally, the larger percentage of career soldiers in the all-volunteer force added to long-term retirement costs.[38]

The Nixon Doctrine placed heavy emphasis on foreign military sales and credit programs in order to promote a more indirect approach to U.S. support of friends and allies providing for their own defense as U.S. conventional forces and capabilities continued to shrink.[39]

Cold War Buildup

Nixon's resignation in 1974 left the new President Gerald Ford, to sustain the Nixon Doctrine.[40] Ford attempted to renew the budget policy battles with Congress but with little success. Ford suffered several veto overrides, leading to a $7.3 billion cut to his 1976 defense budget request, the rejection of his $5 billion cut to domestic programs, and appropriations add-ons of more than $3 billion of nondefense spending bills.[41] Ford completed and released his final FY 1978 defense budget immediately after the November 1976 election, where he continued to seek nuclear force modernization.[42] Like Nixon, Ford's budget addressed each piece of the nuclear triad, theater nuclear systems, and modernization of the Navy's fleet (building a 600 ship active duty fleet--a concept later associated with President Ronald Reagan).

In 1976, Jimmy Carter became President and was faced with the immediate and daunting pressures to make changes to his predecessor's defense program. Carter's campaigned on cutting the defense budget by $7 billion and balancing the budget by

---

[38] Ibid, 345.

[39] Melvin R. Laird, *A Strong Start in a Difficult Decade: Defense Policy in the Nixon-Ford Years,* International Security, 1985, 6.

[40] Ibid., 8.

[41] Dennis S.Ippolito, *"Blunting the Sword: Budget Policy and the Future of Defense,"* (Washington DC, National Defense University, 1994), 22.

[42] Brian J. Auten, *Carter's Conversion The Hardening of American Defense Policy.* (Columbia: University of Missouri Press, 2008), 43.

fiscal year 1981. President Carter's Secretary of Defense Harold Brown believed Carter's

promised reductions should be more moderate, so he proposed cutting $3 billion from the

defense budget believing that would be more acceptable to the service chiefs by slowing

procurement of major weapons systems without terminating them. In the end, the

FY1978 defense budget was revised by $2.8 billion from $123.2 billion to $120.4 billion

a 2.3 percent defense reduction.

Despite being small, Carter's small defense cut was later referred to as a strategic

force "slowdown" because it aimed directly at Ford's nuclear modernization programs.

The B-1 penetrating bomber program was cancelled in favor of Intercontinental Ballistic

Missiles (ICBMs), submarine-launched ballistic missiles (SLBMs), and a fleet of

modernized B-52s armed with air-launched cruise missiles (ALCMs) in reduced numbers

than originally planned. Carter highlighted the   B-1's price tag when he announced the

cancellation of the program, and he explained later in his memoirs that at the time he

believed cruise missiles were more cost-effective than the B-1.[43] Carter also believed

that duplication of weapon systems among services was costing the U.S. government $50

billion or more per year, and he blamed the Joint Chiefs and service rivalry for expensive

hardware. [44]

The Carter administration focused on conventional force modernization in

support of the NATO alliance. On August 24, 1977, Carter signed Presidential

Directive/National Security Council-18, U.S. National Strategy. Carter retained the

national defense strategy of his predecessors of one and a half wars--a major war in

---

[43] Jimmy Carter, *Keeping Faith: Memoirs of a President* (New York: Bantam, 1982), 80-83.
[44] Mark Perry, *Four Stars*, (Boston: Houghton Mifflin, 1989), 267.

Europe and a minor war in Asia (Korea), and unlike his predecessors Nixon and Ford,

Carter made no reductions in Army force structure dedicated to NATO. [45]

In 1979, Carter initiated defense spending increases for 1980 and beyond to

counter Soviet military spending and in response to their aggression in Afghanistan, the

Iranian hostage crisis, and the needs of NATO allies.[46] During his 1980 reelection bid,

President Carter began campaigning on promises to increase defense spending through

1985 to rebuild the military after years of declining defense budgets.[47] President Carter's

opponent, Ronald Reagan, took an aggressive position on defense and attacked him for

weakening the nation's defense to an all time low as the Soviet Union continued to invest

in their strategic and conventional arms.[48]

The Reagan Buildup

When Reagan took office he immediately increased Carter's defense spending

program and proposed a five-year plan to raise the defense budget share by over 60

percent and the defense GNP share by more than 30 percent.[49] Reagan was unable to shift

budget policy to the extent of his proposal, but he did succeed in raising defense spending

significantly. Under Reagan defense spending focused on strengthening the military's

posture in the areas of strategic forces, combat readiness, force mobility, and general

---

[45] M. Glenn Abernathy, Dilys M. Hill, and Phil Williams, *The Carter Years: The President and Policy Making,* (*New York*: St. Martin's Press, 1984), 115.

[46] Jimmy Carter, *Budget Message to the Congress Transmitting the Fiscal Year 1981 Budget,* (Washington, DC: The White House, January 28, 1980), http://www.presidency.ucsb.edu/ws/?pid=32851 (accessed March 23, 2013).

[47] Ibid.

[48] Jungkun Seo, "The Party Politics of Guns Versus Butter in Post-Vietnam America," *Journal of American Studies* 45, no. 2: 317-336.

[49] Dennis S. Ippolito, *Blunting the Sword: Budget Policy and the Future of Defense,* (Washington, DC, National Defense University, 1994), 25.

purpose forces along with modernizing the nation's strategic bomber, submarine and land-based missile systems despite a stagnant economy.[50]

On March 23, 1983, Reagan proposed the Strategic Defense Initiative (SDI) largely known in the mainstream media as "Star Wars" to counter the Soviet missile threat by intercepting and destroying strategic ballistic missiles before they reached the United States. SDI was never truly developed or deployed, though certain aspects of SDI research and technologies paved the way for today's theater missile defense (where the scope centers more on regional coverage vice global).[51]

The high water mark for defense spending during President Regan's Cold War buildup was FY 1985 when defense spending reached $561 billion, an increase of 51 percent over the previous low in FY 1975 and 41 percent over the FY 1980 level.[52] The Reagan buildup included funding increases in all appropriations. Procurement increased by 157 percent, research and development by 98 percent, military construction and family housing by 84 percent, operations and maintenance by 62 percent, and military personnel by 13 percent.[53] Reagan's national defense strategy placed emphasis on both strategic and conventional forces. The Reagan buildup allowed for significant increases in each of the services. The Air Force increased by 71 percent to $193 billion, Navy by 58 percent to $187 billion, Army by 57 percent to $152 billion, and Defense-Wide activities by 37

---

[50] Richard Reeves, *President Reagan: The Triumph of Imagination.* (New York: Simon & Schuster, 2005), 133.

[51] Strategic Defense Initiative Organization (U.S.). Report to the Congress on the Strategic Defense Initiative, Washington, D.C., 1985.

[52] U.S. Department of Defense. Department of Defense Budget Estimates 2012. http://comptroller.defense.gov/defbudget/fy2013/budget_justification/index.html (assessed Febuary 5, 2013).

[53] Ibid.

percent to $54 billion. Military manpower increased by 11 percent including a 4 percent increase in ground forces. [54]

By Reagan's second term public support for defense increases were beginning to wane in support of deficit control and domestic programs. Deficits reaching nearly $150 billion annually in Reagan's first term forced the President and Congress to a compromise that became known as the Gramm-Rudman-Hollings bill.[55] This bill established annual deficit ceilings designed to bring the budget into balance over a 6-year period. If the projected deficit for an upcoming fiscal year was above the ceiling then the President and Congress were required to eliminate the excess deficit through additional taxes or spending cuts. If they failed to do so, automatic spending cuts (sequesters) were to be applied to nonexempt spending programs which meant defense and discretionary domestic accounts.[56]

The cuts between defense and domestic programs were to be apportioned on a roughly 50-50 basis. In the end, this approach failed to prevent large budget deficits and all sides continued to protect their priorities of tax and entitlement programs, but it essentially stalled Reagan's defense buildup. In FY 1985 Reagan believed the defense buildup had made significant progress toward achieving the nation's defense strategy and began making modest reductions in defense spending.[57]

---

[54] U.S. Department of Defense. Department of Defense Budget Estimates 2012. http://comptroller.defense.gov/defbudget/fy2013/budget_justification/index.html (assessed Febuary 5, 2013).
[55] Ippolito, 29.
[56] Stanley E. Collender. *The Guide to the Federal Budget*. (Washington, D.C., Urban Institute Press, 1985), 33.
[57] Ippolito, 30.

Year	Army	Air Force	Navy	Marine Corps	Total
1985	780,787	601, 515	570, 705	198, 025	2, 151, 032

Active Duty Military Personnel 1985 (Source: Department of Defense)

Post-Cold War Transition

The 1988 presidential election appeared to ensure continuity in defense policy. In 1989 George H.W. Bush came into office with the intent of pursuing small increases in defense spending. President Bush had endorsed the Reagan buildup, pledging to support strategic force modernization and to correct the conventional force imbalance. There was an expectation that Bush would press Congress to increase defense spending; however, the Soviet bloc dissolved within the first two years of Bush taking office and the Soviet Union dissolved towards the end of his third year in office.[58] The Omnibus Budget Reconciliation Act of 1990 prohibited spending transfers from defense to domestic programs for 3 years. The 1990 budget agreement provided short-term protection for the defense budget; however, limits on discretionary spending had the unintended effect of making defense more vulnerable to future cuts.[59] With the diminished Soviet threat, President Bush proposed significant defense cuts in his FY 1991 budget. In March 1990, President Bush announced a new national security strategy which stated the U.S. would still contribute to the global balance of power but would make its "military forces smaller, more agile, and better suited to likely contingencies.[60] The 1991 the planned defense reductions were delayed as the US and its allies conducted Operations Desert

---

[58] George Bush and Brent Scowcroft. *A World Transformed.* (New York: Knopf, 1998), 260.
[59] Ippolito, 39.
[60] Gerhard Peters and John T. Woolley, "George Bush: Statement on Transmitting the Annual National Security Strategy Report, March 20, 1990," The American Presidency Project
http://www.presidency.ucsb.edu/ws/index.php?pid=18270&st=national+security
(accessed February 5, 2013).

Shield/Desert Storm to drive Iraqi forces out of Kuwait (August 1990-Febuary 1991).

Much of the cost for Desert Shield/Desert Storm was significantly defrayed by coalition

partners, so US defense spending only increased by 1 percent during this period.[61]

Following the end of the Gulf War in 1991, the nation's plan to achieve a peace

dividend through defense reductions was underway. The president began recommending

base closing under Base Realignment and Closure (BRAC) along with shifting the

nation's focus away from global confrontation to regional threats and diplomatic

engagements built around a significantly smaller and capable military force.[62]

Meanwhile, Governor Bill Clinton, President Bush's 1992 presidential opponent,

campaigned on expanding domestic programs by making significant cuts in the defense

budget and transforming the military for the post-Cold War world. [63]

Post-Cold War

Bill Clinton, the first post-Cold War president, announced his administration

would pursue defense reductions of at least $88 billion. Upon taking office, President

Clinton proceeded to reduce the defense budget and transform the military for the post-

Cold War world.[64] During a "Bottom-Up Review" President Clinton directed that the

"Armed Forces be ready to face two major regional conflicts occurring almost

simultaneously," however, the only major changes "were a further increment of budget

---

[61] House Budget Committee, Update on Costs of Desert Shield/Desert Storm: Hearing Before the Committee on the Budget, 102nd Cong., 1st Sess., May 15, 1991.

[62] Richard J. Samuels, Encyclopedia of United States National Security, Thousand Oaks, Calif: Sage Publications, 2006, 27.

[63] Gerhard Peters and John T. Woolley, "William J. Clinton: Address Before a Joint Session of Congress on Administration Goals," The American Presidency Project, http://www.presidency.ucsb.edu/ws/index.php?pid=47232&st=defense&st1=#axzz1livuk65I (accessed March 15, 2013).

[64] Andrew Feickert and Stephen Daggett, A Historical Perspective on Hollow Forces, Congressional Research Service, 2012. <http://www.fas.org/sgp/crs/natsec/R42334.pdf>.

and personnel reductions, shared evenly across the services."[65] By 1994, with training, readiness and quality of life his top defense priorities, President Clinton objected to further reductions in defense and proposed a slight increase in defense spending and BRAC recommendations to Congress.[66] The military's challenge of operating with reduced funding was exacerbated when it had used its base budget to fund contingency operations in the Persian Gulf, Somalia, Rwanda, Haiti, and elsewhere.[67] Later that year when facing significant pressure to balance the budget for FY 1996, President Clinton compromised with Congress to fund Bosnia operations with the base budget, putting further pressure on defense spending.[68] By FY 1997 and through FY 1998, President Clinton's defense reductions went too far for Congress which provided the DoD with more defense spending than the president requested.[69]

Even with congressional additions, defense spending reached a post-Cold War low in FY 1998 at $375 billion, an amount on par with previous drawdowns.[70] However, the Cold War buildup was different from the Korean and Vietnam War buildups, as the nation only increased its armed forces 10 percent during the Cold War.[71] While the nation reduced defense spending 33 percent during the Cold War drawdown, the DoD reduced its manpower levels by 37 percent and leveraged procurement funding which it

---

[65] Ibid.
[66] Gerhard Peters and John T. Woolley, "William J. Clinton: Address Before a Joint Session of Congress on Administration Goals," The American Presidency Project, http://www.presidency.ucsb.edu/ws/index.php?pid=47232&st=defense&st1=#axzz1livuk65I (accessed March 15, 2013).
[67] Ibid.
[68] Ibid.
[69] Ibid.
[70] Ibid.
[71] Ibid.

reduced by 65 percent.[72] The DoD managed smaller reductions in operations and

maintenance, research and development, military construction and family housing.[73]

As defense spending dropped 33 percent, the DoD disproportionately reduced the

military service funding (i.e., Air Force by 44 percent, Army by 39 percent and the Navy

and Marine Corps by 38 percent) to decrease Defense-Wide spending by 10 percent.[74]

Prior to the Cold War buildup, DoD allocated 32 percent to the Navy and Marine Corps,

31 percent to the Air Force, 26 percent to the Army and 11 percent for Defense-Wide

activities.[75] Following the Cold War drawdown, Defense-Wide activities consumed 15

percent ($56 billion) of the defense budget, more than one-half the 25 percent ($93

billion) for the Army and 29 percent ($109 billion) for the Air Force.[76] From a Major

Force Program perspective, the DoD cut strategic forces the most (82 percent) and took

significant reductions in general purpose forces (44 percent) and mobility forces (41

percent) to minimize reductions in National Guard and Reserve Forces (9 percent) and

Special Operations Forces (11 percent).[77]

Even though defense spending was at a low in FY 1998, the DoD continued

reducing its manpower through FY 2001.[78] During the Cold-War drawdown, the DoD

reduced its manpower by 37 percent, an average of 3 percent a year, bottoming out at 2.1

million total DoD employees (1.5 million military and 687, 000 civilians). The DoD

reduced its military services by similar percentages (i.e., Air Force 42 percent, Army 39

---

[72] Ibid.
[73] Andrew Feickert and Stephen Daggett, A Historical Perspective on Hollow Forces,
Congressional Research Service, 2012. <http://www.fas.org/sgp/crs/natsec/R42334.pdf>. (assessed January
15, 2012).
[74] Ibid.
[75] Ibid.
[76] Ibid.
[77] Ibid.
[78] Ibid.

percent, Navy 37 percent) except for the Marine Corps which was reduced 14 percent from 200,000 to 173, 000 Marines.[79] While the DoD reduced its civilian workforce by 39 percent, it leveraged civilian reductions within the services (Army 47 percent, Navy 45 percent, and Air Force 41 percent) and minimizes reductions in the Defense-Wide civilian workforce by 31 percent.[80]

The Cold-War drawdown went too far for some national policy makers. In submitting the FY 1999 Budget, President Clinton asked Congress to provide additional defense funding to "reverse the decline in defense spending that began in 1985."[81] Congress, however, continued providing additional defense spending through FY 2001 which went beyond President Clinton's budget requests.[82]

Global War on Terror and Beyond

Governor George W. Bush campaigned on establishing a "humble" foreign policy, meaning the direct opposite of Bill Clinton's interventionism. Governor Bush pledged to focus on "enduring national interests" rather idealistic humanitarian goals. In his campaign speeches Governor Bush warned against the notion of using the military option in every difficult foreign policy situation or as a substitute for strategy.[83] In his first budget following the 2000 election, President Bush requested a pay raise for military service members and increased research and development to begin transforming the military for emerging threats. President Bush also set priorities to use the inherited budget

---

[79] Ibid.

[80] Ibid.

[81] Peters and Woolley, "William J. Clinton: Address Before a Joint Session of Congress on Administration Goals," The American Presidency Project, http://www.presidency.ucsb.edu/ws/index.php?pid=47232&st=defense&st1=#axzz1livuk65I (accessed March 15, 2013).

[82] Ibid.

[83] Philip H. Gordon, "The End of the Bush Revolution," *Foreign Affairs* 85, no. 4 (July - August, 2006): 76.

surplus from the Clinton administration to cut taxes, improve education, fix Medicare and

Social Security, and pay down the national debt.[84] He also described a strategy to

transform the military, take advantage of revolutionary technologies and redefine how

wars would be fought to get the best value for the American taxpayer[85] However, the

attacks on September 11, 2001, altered the prevailing trend in defense spending with

national security emerging as a top national priority.

President Bush obtained emergency supplemental funding to prosecute the Global

War on Terror and signed into law the Authorization for Use of Military Force, and

authorized the mobilization of reserve forces. On October 7, 2001, the U.S. began

Operation Enduring Freedom in Afghanistan. The War on Terror would expand,

increasing defense spending for the next decade.[86] The U.S. increased defense spending

by 12 percent from $409 billion within the first year (FY 2001), $460 billion in FY 2002;

and, defense spending was increased another 18 percent in FY 2003 as Operation Iraqi

Freedom began on March 19, 2003. [87] On average defense spending continued to

increase about 4 percent annually to support operations in Iraq; however, spending in Iraq

changed as the strategy changed in 2007 to address the sectarian violence. President

Bush surged an additional 30,000 ground troops to help stabilize Iraq to address the

---

[84] Gerhard Peters and John T. Woolley, "George W. Bush, Statement on Senate Action on Federal Budget Legislation," The American Presidency Project. http://www.presidency.ucsb.edu/ws/?pid=45683. (assessed March 18, 2013) .

[85] Gerhard Peters and John T. Woolley, "George W. Bush, Remarks at the Swearing-In Ceremony for Donald H. Rumsfeld as Secretary of Defense," The American Presidency Project. http://www.presidency.ucsb.edu/ws/index.php?pid=45725&st=defense&st1=#axzz1livuk65I (assessed March 18, 2013) .

[86] Gerhard Peters and John T. Woolley, "George W. Bush, Address to the Nation Announcing Strikes Against Al Qaida Training Camps and Taliban Military Installations in Afghanistan," The American Presidency Project. http://www.presidency.ucsb.edu/ws/?pid=65088, (assessed March 20, 2013)
.

[87] U.S. Department of Defense, Department of Defense Budget Estimates 2012. http://comptroller.defense.gov/defbudget/fy2013/budget_justification/index.html (assessed Febuary 5, 2013).

violence; defense spending increased another 10 percent in FY 2007 and 8 percent in FY 2008, peaking at $717 billion.[88]

In 2009, a newly elected President Barack Obama inherited two wars and a defense budget at levels not seen since World War II. President Obama decided to shift emphasis away from Iraq and put it towards Afghanistan. President Obama's Afghanistan strategy sent an additional 30,000 troops to Afghanistan that the Congressional Budget Office estimated would cost an additional $36 billion. By FY 2010, defense spending was at $713 billion, 90 percent above the post-Cold War low of $375 billion in FY 1998.[89]

On December 15, 2011, the U.S. marked the official end of the war in Iraq, and forces in Afghanistan are expected to end their combat role in FY 2014, continuing in a training and advisory role post 2014. As the United States enters the post Iraq/Afghanistan era, over decade since the surpluses of the Clinton administration, it has been noted by political and military leaders that the U.S. cannot afford to keep military spending at these historic highs. As the current military drawdown gets underway, the overarching question is how far the nation will reduce defense spending and what lessons from previous drawdowns should be applied in order to avoid the hollowing effect?

Chapter 2 looked back at the post-World War II period and beyond where presidents faced economic and fiscal challenges and sought to bring defense spending into balance as they faced possible budget deficits and war drawdowns. The chapter showed how past Presidents made decisions based on a number of factors including the threats the U.S. faced at the time. The question facing President Obama and Congress-- how much to spend on defense in times of large deficits or in the final years of a war--is

---

[88] Ibid.

[89] Ibid.

not new, Figure 1 shows that a number of presidents have faced similar economic and fiscal circumstances since the end of World War II. For example, Eisenhower began his presidency with the long pursuit of balancing between fiscal responsibility and the proper level of defense for the U.S. Achieving a balanced budget was a priority for Eisenhower, despite the Cold War and despite calls for tax cuts. He understood the need to prepare to fight the next war and not the last. With this and other lessons in mind it is necessary for political and military leaders to examine past drawdowns in order to be historically informed in their strategic approach to planning the future force.

CHAPTER 3: APPROACHES TO PLANNING THE FUTURE FORCE

Overview

Since World War II there has been a great deal of movement in the defense posture of the United States. The United States knows too well the disasters that can result from an under-funded "hollow" force as experienced by Task Force Smith in Korea and the post-Vietnam 70's military force; which lent to a renewed determination to rebuild the force in the 1980's, and the defense challenges of the post-Cold War era. Now as the United States enters the Post-9/11 era and transitions from a decade of war, a complex and uncertain security and fiscal environment awaits the country's leaders (both civilian and military). As the services begin to posture for the future, they face fundamental questions about their identities, their roles, and their capabilities.

In designing the military force of the future to support U.S. national interests and security demands, senior political and military leaders will have to answer critical questions as they are deciding on the best approaches. The first question is, what are U.S. national interests that need to be protected by not only the military instrument of power, but the other elements (Diplomatic, Information, and Economic) as well? Then specific to the military, what strategy is needed to support those national interests? Finally, what is the required force structure? Underlying this ends—ways—means discussion are the questions of risk--likelihood of success or potential for failure--and just how much military force structure can the U.S. afford?

Strategic Guidance

The United States Government generates a number of strategic documents related to national security including the National Security Strategy (NSS), which serves as the

27

grand strategy document for the United States and is intended to provide direction for all government agencies and guide the application of national power (diplomatic, informational, military, and economic). In his 2010 NSS, President Obama wrote that "to achieve the world we seek, the U.S. must apply our strategic approach in pursuit of four enduring national interests:

1. The security of the United States, its citizens, and U.S. allies and partners.

2. A strong, innovative, and growing U.S. economy in an open international economic system that promotes opportunity and prosperity.

3. Respect for universal values at home and around the world.

4. An international order advanced by U.S. leadership that promotes peace, security, and opportunity through stronger cooperation to meet global challenges."[1]

The National Military Strategy (NMS) provides strategic direction on how the Joint Force should align the military ends, ways, means, and risks consistent with the goals established in the NDS and the Quadrennial Defense Review (QDR). These documents are not intended to stand on their own, but are instead designed to work together in order to provide "nested" strategic guidance for the military instruments of the U.S. national security apparatus in coordination and collaboration with the other elements of national power. The QDR is a congressionally-mandated activity that occurs every four years and requires the Secretary of Defense to conduct a review that includes a comprehensive examination of the defense strategy, force structure, force modernization plans, infrastructure, budget plan, and other elements of the defense program and

---

[1] Barack Obama, *National Security Strategy*, Washington, D.C..: US Government Printing Office, May 2011, 7.

policies.[2] The most recent QDR was released in February 2010, and less than 24 months later the abrupt change in the strategic environment was such that President Obama saw the need to produce a non-congressionally mandated defense strategy review.

On January 5, 2012, President Obama officially released *Sustaining U.S. Global Leadership: Priorities for 21st Century Defense* that is designed to provide strategic guidance for the Department of Defense over the next 10 years observing that the U.S. is transitioning from a decade of war. The Defense Strategic Guidance (DSG) was intended to develop and codify a "smart set of strategic priorities" that can be implemented from a position of strength, while acknowledging that growth in the defense budget will slow in future years. The DSG is focused on the military lever of national power in achievement of national interests, and seeks to maintain the strongest military in the world while shifting the overall focus from winning today's wars to preparing for future challenges. Specifically, the DoD will require capabilities and additional investments in order to successfully accomplish the following ten missions:

---

[2] 104th Congress, Section 923 of Public Law 104-201, *National Defense Authorization Act,* 1997, http://www.nps.gov/legal/laws/104thth/104-201.pdf (assessed April 20, 2013).

Counter Terrorism and Irregular Warfare to disrupt, dismantle and defeat al Qaeda
Deter and Defeat Aggression by any potential adversary
Project Power Despite Anti-Access/Area Denial (A2AD) Challenges
Counter Weapons of Mass Destruction
Operate Effectively in Cyberspace and Space
Maintain a Safe, Secure, and Effective Nuclear Deterrent
Defend the Homeland and Provide Support to Civil Authorities
Provide a Stabilizing Presence Abroad, Including Rotational Deployments and Bilateral and Multilateral Training Exercises
Conduct (Limited) Stability and Counterinsurgency Operations
Conduct Humanitarian, Disaster Relief, and Other Operations

Table 1. Missions Required by the Defense Strategy Guidance[3]

These missions will form the basis for future force structure and forward basing

decisions. For example, consider that the DSG's force sizing guidance is a departure from

the previous' "Two Major Theater War" (2MTW) strategic construct, and instead directs

that the Joint Force will be capable of fully denying "a capable state's aggressive

objectives in one region…while denying the objectives of--or imposing unacceptable

costs on--an opportunistic aggressor in a second region."[4] The 2MTW construct was

designed to ensure the U.S. the had necessary force structure to fight and win two nearly

simultaneous major theater wars in the Middle East and in the Asia–Pacific region. This

change in force sizing guidance is the result of an assessment that the joint force is

unlikely to find itself simultaneously facing two "capable states," at least for the

foreseeable future. (It also provides general justification for reducing land forces.)

The DSG further directs that "U.S. forces will no longer be sized to conduct large-

scale, prolonged stability operations" along the lines of the recent wars in Iraq and

Afghanistan.[5] This change is consistent with the mission to conduct limited

counterinsurgency and other stability operations. Given the nation's decade long

---

[3] Author generated table. Missions excerpted from, Department of Defense, *Sustaining Global Leadership: Priorities for 21st Century Defense*, Dept of Defense, Washington, DC.:January 2012, 4. http://www.defense.gov/news/defense_strategic_guidance.pdf
[4] Ibid.
[5] Ibid., 6

involvement in these types of manpower-intensive operations that rarely yield decisive wins, there is little appetite to pursue them in the future. Consider former-Secretary of Defense Robert Gates statement, "In my opinion, any future defense secretary who advises the president to again send a big American land army into Asia or into the Middle East or Africa should 'have his head examined,' as General MacArthur so delicately put it."[6]

The changes in the security environment that prompted the publication of updated guidance were numerous and include:

- The death of Osama bin Laden in May 2011;

- The U.S. withdrawal of all combat forces from Iraq in December 2011 and its plans to withdraw combat troops from Afghanistan by the end of 2014;

- The "Arab Spring", a revolutionary wave of demonstrations, protests, and civil unrest in the Arab world that began on December 18, 2010, has changed the entire political landscape in the Middle East; whereas the results of which may not be fully known until sometime in the distant future;

- The global economic crisis and the U.S. national debt that former Chairman of the Joint Chiefs of Staff Admiral Mike Mullen called "the greatest threat to our national security"; [7]

---

[6] Robert M. Gates, Commencement Address, United States Military Academy Graduation, West Point, NY, February 25, 2011. http://www.defense.gov/speeches/speech.aspx?speechid=1539 (assessed April 21, 2013).

[7] Roxana Tiron, "Joint Chiefs chairman reiterates security threat of high debt," *The Hill*, http://thehill.com/homenews/administration/105301-mullen-reiterates-threat-excessive-debt-poses-to-nation (assessed June 10, 2013).

- China's continued rise and increasing geopolitical tensions resulting in growing assertiveness in the resource-rich South China Sea;

- Positive signs of political reforms in Burma; North Korean President Kim Jong Il's death and the transition of power to his son, Kim Jong Un; and continued concerns about Iran's nuclear program.

At a minimum, strategy is designed to link ends (national interests) ways (concepts that describe how something might be done), and means (resources that are employed as capabilities). Additionally, force planners seek to identify, and mitigate, the risk that results from a mismatch between ends, ways and means. Given the current state of the U.S. economy, there is little doubt that fewer defense resources will be available for the foreseeable future as the U.S. plan the forces needed to implement its strategy.

Ever since the end of the Cold War, the U.S. has struggled to gain consensus on an appropriate force planning methodology and answer the question "how much is enough" concerning the size of its military. This was the principle topic of the first QDR and the National Defense Panel's (NDP) Alternative Force Structure Assessment, and remains an important task for the U.S. force planners today and most likely for future QDRs.[8]

Force Planning

Since the Cold War, military planners have used two very different force-planning methodologies in an attempt to determine the right military forces. Threat-based planning was the principled method employed to size U.S. forces during the Cold War. The threat approach involves identifying potential opponents and assessing their capabilities. This

---

[8] Henry C. Bartlett, "The Art of Strategy and Force Planning," *Naval War College Review*, (Spring 1995), 114.

methodology is preeminent when threats to U.S. interests are easily recognized and identified as was the case in the post-World War II environment with the Soviet Union. The dynamic nature of the security environment today makes the threat approach to force planning more problematic since the threats are not as obvious as they were during the Cold War.

The second major methodology is the capabilities approach which concentrates on evolving operational challenges such as the ability of potential adversaries to deny access to theaters of operations using a range of weapons systems. This methodology does not focus on a specific opponent or a single threat, but claims to focus on objectives rather than scenarios. Forces are sized either with a resource constraint emphasis (budget driven), or by focusing on generic military missions required to protect U.S. interests[9]

	Strategy	Scenario (focus)	Leading Methodology	Supporting Effort
Eisenhower 1950s	New Look (nuclear war-fighting)	Strategic nuclear war with the Soviet Union	Capabilities-based (resource variant)	
Kennedy/ Johnson 1960s	Flexible Response (2 and 1/2 wars)	Monolithic Communist threat •Central Europe against Soviet Union •Asia against China •Lesser contingency	Threat-based	Specialized capabilities for intervention operations
Nixon/Ford/ Carter 1970s	1 and 1/2 wars	•War in Central Europe •Lesser contingency	Threat-based	Rapid deployment capabilities (RDJTF)
Reagan 1980s	Horizontal escalation	•Global war with Soviet Union •Possibly triggered by Soviet invasion of Iran	Threat-based	Continued development of rapid deployment capabilities

Figure 2. Cold War Force Planning[10]

Alternative Approaches to Force Planning

The central challenge today for the U.S. leaders is planning under uncertainty. As the U.S. transitions from a decade of war and readjusts its defense strategy for future

---

[9] Ibid., 32.
[10] Ibid.

threats, alternative approaches to force planning, as outlined in Table 3, will have to be considered and applied so as to properly posture the U.S. over the next decade and quarter century, where the regular and irregular threats and opportunities may become even more difficult to identify and defend against.

Approaches	Drivers	Strengths	Pitfalls
Top-Down	Interests Objectives Strategies	Systematic focus on ends; Integrates tools of power; Descriptors lend focus	Constraints considered later; Possibly inflexible; Lack of detail about executability
Bottom-Up	Existing Capability	Practical current focus; Emphasizes real world; Improves existing forces	Present emphasized over future; Neglects long-term creativity; Neglects integrated global view
Scenario	Specific situations	Tangible focus; Encourages priorities; Dynamic-treats time well	World unpredictable; May take on "a life of its own"; Limited insights on longer timeline
Threat and Vulnerability	Risk Adversaries Own weak points	Focus on potential adversaries; both broad and specific focus; Emphasizes force capabilities	Identification contentious; Reactive; Biased toward quantitative data
Core Competency, Capability and Missions	Functions	Prioritizes core capabilities; Maximizes strengths; Exploits weaknesses of others	May retain outdated capabilities; May ignore higher-level goals; Tends toward sub-optimization
Hedging	Minimize Risk	Full spectrum of capability; Confronts uncertain future; Seeks balance and flexibility	Understates own strengths; Exaggerates others' capabilities; Very costly
Technology	Dominant systems	Stresses knowledge; Encourages creativity; Creates military leverage	Risks high cost for small gain; May undervalue human factors; may unbalance force structure
Fiscal	Budget	Defense linked to economy; Requires priority setting; Fosters fiscal discipline	May lead to underfunded needs; Tends to create cyclic spending; Leads to "fair sharing"

Table 2. Summary of Alternative Approaches to Force Planning[11]

Strategic Outlook in Planning the Future Force

Both Former Secretary of Defense Robert Gates and Chairman of the Joint Chiefs of Staff General Martin Dempsey have made major speeches outlining the way ahead and

---

[11] Ibid.

their strategic outlook into planning the future force. Both Gates and Dempsey speeches provide a number of key take aways that are pertinent to this research. In Secretary Gates' last policy speech before leaving office, he discussed the reshaping of priorities for the Pentagon and the need to reform the way business is being done (how weapons are chosen, developed/produced, and how the services care for their personnel). Secretary Gates weighed in on the U.S. fiscal woes and how the defense budget is not the cause, however large it may be, but DoD must be part of the solution.[12]

According to Secretary Gates, the U.S. will not see a Cold War-level defense budget, at least as a share of GDP, because America is different in ways as it pertains to the economy, demographics, and the political environment. Secretary Gates made a point in this speech to remind his intended audience of Eisenhower's warning regarding the defense industrial complex, bringing attention to the age of the current inventory and its less than optimal conditions after a decade of fighting two wars. He stated, "Some equipment can be refurbished with life-extension programs, but there is no getting around the fact that others must be replaced."[13]

General Dempsey stated shortly after being sworn in as Chairman of the Joint Chiefs of Staff, the military was confronting a "strategic inflection point, where the institution fundamentally re-examines itself."[14] Chairman Dempsey has stated publicly that the U.S. military must leverage emerging technologies and capabilities to create Joint Force 2020, the fighting force of the future. He also said at the 2012 Joint Warfighting

---

[12] Robert Gates. "American Enterprise Institute (Defense Spending)," Office of Assistant Secretary of Defense (Public Affairs) Washington, D.C., May 24, 2011. http://www.defense.gov/speeches/speech.aspx?speechid=1570 (assessed March 22, 2013).

[13] Ibid.

[14] Thom Shanker, "Mapping Military Needs, Aided by a Big Projection," *The New York Times*, September 11, 2012. http://www.nytimes.com/2012/09/12/us/top-general-dempsey-maps-out-us-military-future.html?_r=0 (assessed April 15, 2013).

Conference, "We're transitioning from a decade of war, a complex and uncertain security environment looms, and as we look toward the future each service in our total joint force faces fundamental questions about their identities, their roles and their capabilities."[15] The chairman explained the challenge as a "security paradox" and highlighted the following changes in the security environment that will present challenges to planning the future force: threats as the result of technology proliferation, the shrinking gap in capabilities, and the perishable opportunity to be innovative (procurement, technology, doctrine, training, education, etc.).[16] General Dempsey does believe about 80 percent of Joint Force 2020 already exists today and the major building blocks of today's force will still be around in eight years.[17]

Every war the United States has fought has been different from the last, and different from what defense planners had envisioned. For example, the majority of the bases and facilities used by the United States and its coalition partners in Operation Desert Storm were built in the 1980s, when it was envisioned a Soviet invasion through Iran to be the principal threat to the Gulf region.[18] In planning forces capable of fighting and winning major regional conflicts, the U.S. must avoid preparing for the past wars. History suggests that we most often deter the conflicts that we plan for and actually fight the ones we do not anticipate. Choosing the right methodology to develop the forces for the future involves a number of important factors that must be considered, but most of all

---

[15]Tyrone C. Marshall, "Dempsey Describes Future Force at Warfighting Conference," American Forces Press Service, May 16, 2012. http://www.defense.gov/News/NewsArticle.aspx?ID=116362 (assessed April 5, 2012).

[16] Ibid.

[17] Ibid.

[18] Les Aspin. *Report on the Bottom-Up Review*. U.S. Dept. of Defense, October 1993, Federation of American Scientists Website. http://www.fas.org/man/docs/bur/part03.htm (assessed April 15, 2013).

it requires the nation's leaders to have a clear sense of the strategic ends, ways, and means to get there.

On three occasions in 2012, General Dempsey and all the regional combatant commanders assembled at Marine Corps Base Quantico for what was named the "Strategic Seminar." A basketball court size map of the world was laid on the ground in order to "walk the world." During the daylong sessions military leaders worked their way through a series of potential realistic national security scenarios in order to debate the kind of military--its size capability--the nation will require in the next five years.[19]

He started the strategic seminar with the goal of trying to build the right military force for five years from now, and not be driven by the budget cycle into a series of year-by-year decisions. The overarching question for these seminars was whether the Pentagon's war plans needed to be rewritten to take into account how the military has been affected by a decade of war in Iraq and Afghanistan, and now by mandated budget reductions even as potential adversaries continue to evolve and rising threats remain.[20]

The major takeaways from the strategic seminar was that if the U.S. found itself in an armed conflict within five years it would likely be due to an attack on America or its territories. It is believed that if an attack occurred against America, it would range from a direct missile attack or an asymmetrical terrorist or cyber-attack which concludes that the American homeland is no longer a sanctuary protected by vast oceans. General Ray Odierno, the Army Chief of Staff "told a public forum sponsored by the magazine

---

[19] Thom Shanker, *Mapping Military Needs.*
[20] Ibid.

37

Foreign Affairs that the seminars reshaped his thinking on the number of troops needed over the coming years." [21]

---

[21] Ibid.

CHAPTER 4: ANALYSIS

The international strategic landscape of the twenty-first century is shaped by complex and contradictory forces. The world is characterized by turmoil, and changing patterns of state-to-state relationships as well as conflicts within states caused by ethnic, religious, and national differences have become commonplace.[1] International terrorism, drug cartels, and threats created by information-age technology add to the turmoil. In this new environment, U.S. national security policy and priorities have become complicated, often ambiguous, and even inconsistent—not because of immediate threat of major conventional war but rather the unpredictable, uncertain, and confusing characteristics of the international arena. The post 9/11 landscape has clouded the concept and meaning of U.S. national security and foreign policy as the two have become so intertwined. Historically, national security differed from foreign policy in at least two respects: national security purposes were more narrowly focused on security and safety, and national security was primarily concerned with actual and potential adversaries and their use of force, whether overt or covert; which means there was a military emphasis which is not the case for foreign policy. Foreign policy served more of a multidimensional purpose such as preventing conditions detrimental to the U.S. and maintaining relations with other countries to enhance conditions favorable to U.S. national interests. The instruments of foreign policy are primarily diplomatic and political and include a variety of psychological and economic measures.[2] Former Secretary of Defense Robert Gates has warned on a number of occasions against the risk of a "creeping militarization" of U.S.

---

[1] Sam C. Sarkesian, *U.S. National Security: Policymakers, Processes, and Politics* (Boulder: L. Rienner, 1989), 3.
[2] Ibid., 4.

foreign policy, saying the State Department should lead U.S. engagement with other countries, with the military playing a supporting role;[3] however, the U.S. military, ever versatile and ready to confront new security challenges has become the most convenient instrument of national power as strategic challenges, foreign policy, and security problems have become more complex.

The militarization of U.S. foreign policy, through reliance on the military to pursue objectives better achieved by other means has seriously damaged U.S. interests. It has become universally accepted that the Iraq War was plagued with failures, the War on Terror has not made Americans safer, and the economic costs the U.S.'s emphasis on military action and involvement is enormous.[4] The U.S. can no longer afford to view national security and foreign policy through the narrow lens of the military being the sole protector of U.S. interests.

Over the next decade, the U.S. will have to make the most significant shift in its strategy since Truman's introduction to the nuclear bomb. Defense budgets are declining in the midst of a security environment that seemingly includes the expansion of U.S. interests requiring military power support and protection. This means that tough strategic choices will have to be made since the U.S. no longer has the resources to do everything.[5]

Today, the U.S. military remains the strongest, the most ready, and the most capable in the world; however, current U.S. political and military leaders are debating

---

[3] Ann Scott Tyson, "Gates Warns of Militarized Policy; Defense Secretary Stresses Civilian Aspects of U.S. Engagement," *The Washington Post*, July 16, 2008 (assessed May 29, 2001).

[4] Mitchell, David and Tansa George Massoud, "Anatomy of Failure: Bush's Decision-Making Process and the Iraq War." *Foreign Policy Analysis* 5, no. 3 (2009): 265-86.. http://onlinelibrary.wiley.com/doi/10.1111/j.1743-8594.2009.00093.x/pdf (assessed May 15, 2013).

[5] Robert Gates, "Hearing to Receive Testimony on the Challenges Facing the Department of Defense," January 27, 2009, http://www.armed-services.senate.gov/Transcripts/2009/01%20January/A%20Full%20Committee/09-02%20-%201-27-09.pdf (assessed May 15, 2013).

how much is enough to spend on defense under current budget constraints. This chapter attempts to analyze and apply lessons of past strategic direction where cuts were imposed and defense challenges were realized, in order to make recommendations on how to shape and size the force of the future.

National Interests

National interests can be considered a set of shared priorities which are influence by a variety of factors. U.S. national interests have been shaped in part by historical, cultural, geographical, demographical, technological, sociological, economic, and natural resource environments.[6] It is generally agreed that the U.S. interests are defined in broad categories: survival, economic welfare and prosperity, preservation of the national value system at home, and projection of national values overseas. In prioritizing those interests, national survival is naturally paramount. Moreover, for the U.S. during the Cold War, national survival was believed to be under serious threat from the Soviet Union. Thus when other categories of national interests appeared to clash with policies dictated by the national survival interest, those secondary interests were invariably ignored or deemphasized.[7]

Today, while national survival must remain the highest priority among U.S. national interests, America faces virtually no threat from abroad. U.S. economic welfare and prosperity, on the other hand, are generally agreed to be gravely threatened, as has been stated by former defense leaders. It is this national interest—and threat to it—that

---

[6] Joseph S. Nye Jr., "Redefining the National Interest," *Foreign Affairs*, 78, no. 4 (July. - August, 1999): 22-23.
    [7] Ibid., 26-27.

41

the American public believes should be the current administration's top priority and should not ignore.[8]

The U.S. environment, international circumstances, domestic politics and the psyche of many actors engaged in international affairs influence the development of American national interests.[9] Trends, such as the information revolution, affect the speed and accuracy of information as well as the movement of capital around the world. Political parties and interest groups offer opinions as to what is considered to be in the national interest. While the Constitution sets foreign affairs under the purview of the executive branch, Congress and the courts have played an increasing role in shaping foreign policy. In addition, government officials are influenced in varying degrees by public opinion as portrayed by the media. Furthermore, all of the actors influencing or acting upon foreign affairs bring a variety of heritage themes, cultures, and personalities into the arena.[10] Given the variety of factors which influence U.S. values, it is not surprising that defining its interests can be a complicated undertaking.

The Role of the Economy in U.S. National Security

> To be a Great Power – by definition, a state capable of holding its own against any other nation – demands a flourishing economic base.[11]

Although there were dangerous moments in the Cold War during the 1950s, people often remember the Eisenhower years as "happy days," a time when Americans did not have to worry about depression or war, as they had in the 1930s and 1940s, or difficult and divisive issues, as they did in the 1960s. Instead, Americans spent their time

---

[8] Gallup, "Most important problem," Gallup, http://www.gallup.com/poll/1675/most-important-problem.aspx (assessed June 4, 2013).
[9] The War Room, "Good Cop, Bad Cop, Consistent US Interests," National Security Network, http://nsnetwork.org/good-cop-bad-cop-consistent-us-interests/ (assessed June 4, 2013).
[10] Ibid.
[11] Paul Kennedy, *The Rise and Fall of Great Powers*, (New York, Random House, 1987), 539.

enjoying the benefits of a booming economy. Over fifty-three years ago, President Dwight D. Eisenhower explained that a nation's security was directly tied to the health of its economy.

The President faced important and, at times, controversial issues in domestic affairs. Managing the economy involved important choices about how to maintain prosperity or how much to spend on what we today call "infrastructure". He also consistently resisted calls from military leaders and some members of Congress to outspend the Soviets.[12]

For several decades following World War II, providing national security was conceptually simple. The U.S. maintained the world's preeminent military backed by the world's largest economy. The conventional wisdom was that the U.S. government could provide security for the nation primarily by keeping the Soviet military at bay and containing their communist ideology. The economy always was there, both to fund the military and underpin the provision of economic security for households.[13]

Not surprisingly, the magnitude of the fiscal crisis today has inevitably evoked warnings that debt and deficits threaten its national security, igniting a debate centered on the federal government's budget in general and military expenditures in particular. The expectation is that the current and projected growth in the national debt is not sustainable and, given the slow recovery from the financial crisis, the U.S. is facing a period of increased austerity that will compel deep cuts in the federal budget. As previously

---

[12]   Andrew F. Krepinevich, Jr., "National Security Strategy in an Era of Growing Challenges and Resource Constraints," *Center for Strategic and Budgetary Assessments Perspective*, June 2010, 6.
   [13] Ibid., 8.

mentioned, in August 2010, Admiral Mike Mullen, Chairman of the Joint Chiefs of Staff, stated that the national debt is the single biggest threat to national security.[14]

In theory, the budget for the national security community, including the military and homeland security, should be sufficient to address foreign threats, defend the homeland, prevail in ongoing wars, and help define and advance U.S. interests abroad, including, to a certain extent, projecting U.S. democratic values and human rights.[15] In practice, there is considerable disagreement on how best to address these tasks and the ways and means necessary to carry them out. One can hardly expect a public policy consensus on the optimal size of the military budget and whether the amount being spent is too great or too small. The line of reasoning in the public debate tends to be that the military budget is either too large or too small relative to what the country can afford, to past expenditures, to overall federal budget, to what is spent on other programs, or to what other nations spend. Another line of reasoning is that the military budget also is too large or too small relative to current war fighting needs, to rising threats from non-state actors or from states with nuclear weapons programs (such as North Korea and Iran), or for its participation in alleviating the effects of natural disasters (such as earthquakes, tsunamis, infectious diseases, or climate change).

The importance of the economy is highlighted in the National Security Strategy which declares that our national power ultimately rests on the strength and resilience of the economy.[16] It is paramount the American people understand the linkages between the

---

[14] Michael Cheek, " Mullen: National Debt is a Security Threat," *Executive Gov*, August 27, 2010, http://www.executivegov.com/2010/08/mullen-national-debt-is-a-security-threat/ (assessed May 31, 2013).

[15] U.S. Department of Defense, *Quadrennial Defense Review Report*, Washington DC.: US Government Printing Office, 2010.

[16] Barack Obama, *National Security Strategy*, Washington, D.C..: US Government Printing Office, May 2011, 9.

U.S. economy and its national security. A strong economy gives a country and its leaders more options in its engagements in the world and it is essential to maintaining a strong military. It is up to the country's leadership to influence the political environment as Eisenhower did to change some of the country's habits that adversely affect its economy, or the U.S. will be unable to develop a national security strategy that will maintain its position of world leadership and influence.

US Defense Spending

Since World War II, the U.S. has annually spent anywhere from 3 to 13 percent of its GDP on the military for security needs, involvement in wars, and/or efforts to stimulate the economy.[17] The federal government has varied its financing strategies through the years conditioned by specific needs prompting increases and decreases in defense spending. For instance, tax hikes or the combination of tax hikes and deficits spending have been employed to support the U.S. military during wars. Such approaches generally have not been politically attractive during peacetime; instead, reducing welfare spending to increase military spending, the so-called gun versus butter trade-off has been a preferred approach under such conditions. On the other hand, some administrations have relied upon a combination of deficit spending and tax cuts, simultaneously targeting the dual goals of supporting the military and stimulating the national economy.[18]

Most Americans believe the U.S. government spends far more on defense than it actually does. Due to the Budget Control Act and sequestration, defense spending has

---

[17] H. Sonmez Atesoglu, "Defense Spending and Aggregate Output in the United States," *Defense and Peace Economics*, 2009, 21-26.

[18] Robert Barro, "Government Spending in a Simple Model of Endogenous Growth," *Journal of Political Economy* 98, no. 5, Part 2, (October 1990): 121-123.

been reduced to unprecedented levels during wartime. [19] The growing disparity between funding and requirements is the primary cause of the increasing strain on the defense budget, but numerous other external and internal factors also are contributing to the problem.

World War II, the Korean War, the Vietnam War, the Cold War, and the attacks on September 11 each prompted sharp increases in defense spending. The resulting defense hikes were necessary because they were preceded by periods of inadequate investment, which produced military shortcomings that were often fully exposed only when troops entered combat. During each war, the bulk of the new spending went toward the specific mix of capabilities required to prevail in the contingency of the day. [20]

After each war-driven boom, the defense budget has experienced an extended period of decline. In May 2007, U.S. Secretary of Defense Robert Gates explained:

> Five times over the past 90 years—after the First and Second World Wars, Korea, Vietnam and most recently after the Cold War--the United States has slashed defense spending or disarmed outright in the mistaken belief that the nature of man or the behavior of nations had changed with the end of each of the wars, or that somehow we would not face threats to our homeland or would not need to take a leadership role abroad. [21]

Time and again, policymakers have tended to sacrifice defense absent immediate, manifest threats to U.S. interests; and Americans and their military personnel have repeatedly paid the price of being less prepared. Political and military leaders should take advantage of peacetime lulls to replace damaged or destroyed equipment, to

---

[19] Jeffrey M. Jones, "Americans Divided in Views of U.S. Defense Spending," *Gallup*, February 21, 2013. http://www.gallup.com/poll/160682/americans-divided-views-defense-spending.aspx (assessed April 30, 2013).

[20] Kevin N. Lewis, "The Disciplined Gap and Other Reasons for Humility and Realism in Defense Planning," *New Challenges for Defense Planning: Rethinking How Much is Enough* (Santa Monica, Calif.: RAND Corporation, 1994), 104.

[21] Robert Gates, "Remarks to the Greater Dallas Chamber of Commerce," May 3, 2007, http://www.defense.gov/transcripts/transcript.aspx?transcriptid=3956 (assessed May 23, 2013).

modernize legacy systems, and to purchase next-generation replacements to avoid predictable shortfalls in future force structure. Yet most administrations have failed to do so.

Procurement Holiday

The "procurement holiday" during the 1990s was carried out with bipartisan support in Congress as the Clinton Administration drastically cut defense spending after the collapse of the Soviet Union in the overly optimistic belief that an era of relative peace would ensue. Purchases of new weapons fell sharply, resulting in a near freeze in development of new planes, ships, and vehicles. The U.S. did not purchase a single tactical fighter jet in 1995. The U.S. military shrank by one-third across the board, and the average ages of most major platforms doubled.[22] The military that went to war in Afghanistan and Iraq after 9/11 and is still deployed today is essentially the military that Ronald Reagan built.

During the 1990s, policy makers chose to invest in service-life extensions of Reagan-era platforms instead of new equipment. This increased the bill for maintenance, repairs, and upgrades but only delayed (and increased) the bill for modernization. Weapons systems can be patched up for only so long before they retire completely. Equipment eventually falls apart, breaks down, or becomes too hazardous and costly to use. The 1990s modernization hiatus merely deferred cost of replacing aging platforms that were built in the 1970s and 1980s--even while the need for replacements remained constant.

---

[22] Congressional Budget Office, *Total Qualities and Unit Procurement Cost Tables 1974-1995*, April 13, 1995, A8. http://www.cbo.gov/publication/18099 (assessed May 20, 2013).

Under President George W. Bush, the defense budget grew significantly after 9/11 terrorist attacks, but the bulk of the increase was consumed by operations in Afghanistan and Iraq. The relentless demands of wartime operations forced the administration to prioritize end strength growth and investment in counterinsurgency capabilities while capping investment in resetting the force and developing new capabilities. As a result, the U.S. military has yet to fully recover from its procurement holidays during the 1990s.

The Costs of Maintaining an Aging Force

In addition to the wartime damage sustained by military equipment, ordinary aging imposes significant costs. As the average age of many planes, ships, vehicles increases, so does the cost of maintaining and repairing them. One example is the KC-135 Stratotanker. Various press reports have discussed the high cost of maintaining this old air refueling platform.[23] These tankers were built during the Eisenhower Administration, and many are more than 50 years old. They are often grounded because of leaks or broken parts, sometimes for weeks as Air Force engineers cannibalize old tankers for spare parts or recreate them from scratch. Old systems like KC-135 tankers are an additional drain on resources because they are less fuel efficient than newer platforms. Another example, revitalizing the aging Abrams tanks and Bradley vehicles will cost an additional $2 billion annually.[24] This is a common theme across the service. Scarce defense funds are being used to maintain repair, upgrade and fuel old platforms that badly need to be replaced by more efficient next-generation systems.

---

[23] Andrea Stone, "Aging Air Force Tankers Fly on Leaky Wings and Prayer," AOL News, February 22, 2010, http://www.aolnews.com/2010/02/22/aging-air-force-tankers-fly-on-leaky-wings-and-prayers/ (assessed May 22, 2013).

[24] Congressional Budget Office, *Long-Term Implications of the Fiscal Year 2010 Defense Budget*, Washington DC.: US Government Printing Office, 2010, 23.

Trade-Off between Defense, Entitlements, and Interest Payments

The most serious single threat the U.S. faces to its national security does not come from foreign threats, but from the pressure on defense spending created by the domestic social and economic trends, and the rising cost of U.S. federal entitlements spending. Mandatory or entitlement outlays increased by 5.1 percent in 2011, and will rise by an average of 4.4 percent annually between 2012 and 2020, compared with an average growth rate of 6.4 percent between 1999 and 2008.[25] They will average 12.3 percent to 13.3 percent of the GDP during FY2012 to FY2020. Defense spending will average only 3.3 percent to 4.3 percent, dropping from peak war year level of 4.7 percent in FY 2010.[26] Defense claimed almost 90 percent of the federal budget during World War II, 70 percent during the Korean War, about 50 percent during Vietnam, and about 30 percent during the Cold War. Today, defense accounts for less than 20 percent of the federal budget and is falling. The defense share of federal spending is so low a percentage of total federal spending, the GDP, and rising entitlement costs, that no feasible amount of cuts in U.S. national security spending can have a major impact on the U.S. deficit and debt problems. President Obama's budget plan is expected to reduce defense spending to just 15.6 percent in FY 2015, before accounting for the effects of health care reform.[27]

The substantial decline in the defense share of the budget largely reflects the dramatic growth of entitlement spending. Entitlements now account for around 65 percent of all federal spending and a record 18 percent of GDP.[28] The three largest

---

[25] Anthony H. Cordesman and Arleigh A. Burke, *The FY2013 Defense Budget, Sequestration, and Growing Strategy-Reality Gap*, Center for Strategic & International Studies, 2012, 2.
[26] Ibid.
[27] U.S. Office of Management and Budget, *Historical Tables, Budget of the United States Government*, Fiscal Year 2012, Washington DC.: US Government Printing Office 2011, 55.
[28] Ibid.

entitlements--Social Security, Medicare, and Medicaid--eclipsed defense spending in 1976 and have been growing ever since. If future taxes are held at historical average, these three entitlements will consume all tax revenues by 2052, leaving no money for the government's primary constitutional obligation: providing for the common defense.[29]

With deficits at record levels and interest payments on the national debt set to rise at a real rate of 13 percent annually over the next 10 years, interest payments could reach $725 billion and exceed defense spending by 2018.[30] With so much of the federal budget allocated to mandatory spending, this administration--like others before it--will increasingly look to national defense as a bill payer. Roughly half of the Obama Administration's $17 billion in government spending cuts for FY 2010 were found in the defense budget. These cuts included reductions in or terminations of 16 major programs and numerous smaller ones.[31] In the researcher's opinion, Defense is often seen by some policy makers as an attractive pot of cash that can be raided with disregard of immediate consequences. In the long run, lower defense spending leads to a smaller force, reduced troop readiness, longer deployments times, less capable weapons systems, and ultimately the defacto or overt abandonment of America's security commitments around the world.

Unsustainable Growth in the Operations and Support Accounts

The portion of the defense budget devoted to operations and support (O&S), which includes the military personnel account and the operations and maintenance (O&M) account, is expected to grow. It is more than double the share allocated to

---

[29] Ibid.

[30] Todd Harrison, *Avoiding a DoD Bailout*, Center for Strategic and Budgetary Assessment, October 2009, 1-3.

[31] D. Andrew Austin and Mindy R. Levit, *Trends in Discretionary Spending*, Congressional Research Service Report for Congress, July 10, 2009, 6.

military modernization.[32] The imbalance stems in large measure from the growing cost of compensating America's all-volunteer force. The cost of paying the military, particularly deferred and in-kind benefits that are often underfunded entitlements is rising unsustainably despite only marginal increases in the number of ground force troops. If these benefits continue to grow while the overall defense budget remains flat, funding them will require taking ever more money from modernization programs to pay personnel.

Military medical programs account for almost half of the recent growth in O&S funding. The CBO estimates that real spending on medical programs will more than double under the Pentagon's current plans from $44 billion in 2009 to $90 billion in 2028, far outpacing inflation in the wider economy. Pharmaceutical spending alone will increase by about 120 percent, direct care costs by more than 90 percent, and the cost of purchased care and contracts by around 125 percent.[33]

Over the past decade, Congress has added new pension benefits which are contributing to rising personnel costs. For example, retirement pay for military personnel who retire after 20 years of service was increased in 2000 from 40 percent back to 50 percent of a servicemember's basic pay (prior to 1986, the 20 year. retirement pension was 50percent of base pay). In addition, the FY 2000 defense authorization bill enacted Tricare for Life, expanding health care coverage for military retirees and their families.[34]

---

[32] Todd Harrison, *Analysis of the FY 2012 Defense Budget*, Center for Strategic and Budgetary Assessment, July 2011, 27-28.
[33] Congressional Budget Office, *Long-term Implications*, 9-16.
[34] Ibid., 11.

The retirement annuity for surviving spouses of servicemembers was also increased from 35 percent to 55 percent of the deceased's retirement pay,[35] and the retirement age for some members of the Reserve Component has been lowered to 60. The costs of these benefits expansions are compounded by the decade series of congressionally authorized military pay increases. As the CBO points out, "higher basic pay today leads to higher projections of future annuities, in turn requiring larger payments today from the military personnel accounts into the retirement fund."[36]

Tying Security Strategy to the US Role in the Global Economy

The US may not face peer threats in the near to mid-term, but it faces a wide variety of lesser threats that make maintaining effective military forces, foreign aid, and other national security programs a vital national security interest. The U.S. does need to reshape its national security planning and strategy to do a far better job of allocating resources to meet these threats. It needs to abandon theoretical and conceptual exercises in strategy that do not focus on detailed force plans, manpower plans, procurement plans, and budgets; and use its resources more wisely. The U.S. still dominates world military spending, but it must recognize that maintaining the U.S. economy is a vital national security interest in a world where growth and development of other nations and regions means that the relative share the US has in the global economy will decline steadily over time, even under the best circumstances. At the same time, US dependence on the security and stability of the global economy will continue to grow indefinitely in the future. Talk of any form of "independence," including freedom from energy imports, is a dangerous myth. The U.S. cannot maintain and grow its economy without strong military

---

[35] Ibid., 12.
[36] Ibid.

forces and effective diplomatic and aid efforts.[37] U.S. military and national security spending already places a far lower burden on the U.S. economy than during the peaceful periods of the Cold War, and existing spending plans will lower that burden in the future. National security spending is now averaging 4 percent and 5 percent of the GDP--in spite of the fact the U.S. has been fighting two wars in Iraq and Afghanistan--versus 6-7 percent during the Cold War.[38]

---

[37] Cordesman and Burke, *The FY2013 Defense Budget*, 20.
[38] Ibid., 42.

CHAPTER 5: RECOMMENDATIONS AND CONCLUSION

President Obama inherited a defense budget at levels not seen since World War II, and with defense at historic highs, there is bipartisan agreement that sensible cuts can be made without damaging the force. President Obama and all his previous and current Secretaries of Defense have promised there would be no hollow force as the U.S. implements the post-9/11 drawdown in a climate where tough budget choices will have to be made; however, a number of service component commanders have begun reducing training and foregoing required maintenance due to the lack of funding. The U.S. Air Force has grounded combat air squadrons in response to forced spending cuts eliminating more than 44,000 flying hours through September 2013.[1] The Air Force's budget for flying hours was reduced by $591 million for the remainder of fiscal 2013, making it impossible to keep all squadrons ready for combat according to an April 5, 2013 memorandum signed by Major General Charles Lyon, Director of Operations for Air Combat Command.[2]

The U.S. Navy has responded to the budget drawdown by canceling or deferring the deployments of six ships on top of canceling required maintenance on six other ships.[3] Military leaders see these as indicators of declining readiness which will eventually lead to a drop in capability. The underlying cause for concern by military

---

[1] Brian Everstine and Marcus Weisgerber. "Reduced Flying Hours Forces USAF To Ground 17 Combat Air Squadrons," *Defense News*, Apr. 8, 2013, http://www.defensenews.com/article/20130408/DEFREG02/304080011/Reduced-Flying-Hours-Forces-USAF-Ground-17-Combat-Air-Squadrons (accessed April 15, 2013).

[2] Ibid.

[3] Eric Durie, "Department of the Navy Response to Sequestration," *Navy Live*, March 2, 2013, http://navylive.dodlive.mil/2013/03/02/department-of-the-navy-response-to-sequestration/ (accessed April 15, 2013).

leaders is the fact that their budgets are immediately impacted with cuts while changes in required commitments are not as fast. The military must secure the proper balance between three separate but closely related dimensions: readiness, modernization and force structure. The author will present recommendations in this chapter that should be considered in an effort to adapt to the fiscally constrained environment and avoid hollowing the force.

Recommendation One: Publish a hybrid of NSC 68 & NSC-162/2 for the Twenty-First Century

The best approach to drawing down military forces without hollowing out the capabilities of the forces that remain is to design a policy that communicates long-term objectives of the U.S. This policy can be used to develop a National Security Strategy and linked sub-strategies (QDR, NMS) that will enable force planners to construct a corresponding military that aligns ends with ways and means. It is without a doubt that both NSC-68 and NSC-162/2 were important documents of their time that aimed at taking the above approach, in the form of a very grand strategy of containment. In short, it is time to publish a national strategy that is a hybrid similar to NSC- 68 and NSC-162/2 for the twenty-first Century.

Since the end of the Cold War, United States security policy has been ambiguous and lacking a clearly defined threat. This ambiguous policy combined with the lack of capacity (and/or will) within the international system to deal effectively with emerging threats and crises have created an expectation for U.S., as the world's sole super power. The international communities' expectations assumes the U.S. will act as the world's police that is ready and able to respond to any and all global threats and crises ranging from Somalia, Kosovo, Iraq, Libya, Iran, and Syria.

The grand strategy of NSC-68 addressed threats to the U.S. and to the West which vanished with the end of the Cold War. However, the idea behind NSC-68, the need for an organized approach to U.S. security policy, remains as valid today as it was after the war or at any other time; however, NSC-68's call for significant unrestrained peacetime military spending is unrealistic in today's fiscal environment, where implementation of NSC-68 more than tripled the American defense budget.[4]

Under President Truman NSC-68 clearly stated U.S. strategic objectives, evaluated the security environment, weighed the risks, and identified missions the military (as well as other elements of national power) would need to accomplish to achieve those objectives. When President Dwight Eisenhower entered office in 1953, he faced a situation in 1953 similar to what the current administration faces today: how to plan for an uncertain future when the stakes are high and there is little consensus on how to deal with a growing and uncertain strategic threat. He was concerned that the national security strategy articulated by NSC-68, committed the U.S. to an engagement strategy that was not economically sustainable in the long term.[5] On October 30, 1953, President Eisenhower formally approved National Security Council Paper No. 162/2 (NSC 162/2). This top secret document made clear that America's nuclear arsenal must be maintained and expanded to meet the communist threat. It also made clear the connection between military spending and a sound American economy.

---

[4] John Lewis Gaddis, *We now know: Rethinking Cold War History* (New York, Oxford University Press), 1997, 84.
[5] Robert Bowie and Richard Immerman, *Waging Peace: How Eisenhower Shaped an Enduring Cold War Strategy*, New York, 1998, 125.

Even if the U.S. and its allies no longer face a Soviet threat, today's situation is proving to be just as dangerous as it was in the early days of the Cold War. In its place, the international community confronts the combined threats of militant radicalism, the proliferation of nuclear, biological, and chemical weapons, and the rise of rogue nations that threaten to use these weapons. Just as the Cold War became a forty-year struggle, the current security environment will prove to be just as enduring. As was the case with NSC-68, it is imperative that the President examine and determine the U.S. national interests and the means the U.S. should employ when those interests are challenged. And just as was the case with NSC-68, it is essential that having identified U.S. national interests and challenges to those interests U.S. political leaders must build consensus and formulate policy in support of national security objectives.

Recommendation Two: Know that the next war the U.S. will fight will probably not be the one it was preparing to fight

What history shows is that the war the U.S. is prepared to fight is not the war that it inevitably fight. The U.S. military of 1990 was ready to fight in the defense of Western Europe, but an offensive campaign in the Middle East was completely unexpected. As late as 2004, the U.S. military was still trying to fight conventional campaigns in Iraq and Afghanistan with insurgencies continuing to gain momentum as the conflict progressed. These most recent conflicts along with the security and stability operations of the 1990's should set expectations that conflicts of the future will be irregular or along the similar lines.

Future war characteristics will differ sharply from today's wars and the U.S. will need to maintain the basic building blocks of a broad-based military capability that can respond to new and unexpected threats, as well as to the threats that the U.S. faces today.

Since the Cold War, the U.S's defense strategy has relied on overpowering foes not with more troops but more advanced weapons. That advantage helped the U.S. prevail in both Gulf Wars, Afghanistan, and the hunt for Osama bin Laden. The U.S.'s technological advantage will take a conscious effort to maintain. China and Russia are examining asymmetrical military capabilities to exploit U.S. vulnerabilities that will persist in the absence of modernization programs. For example, China is seeking anti-satellite weapons to exploit the vulnerability of U.S. military satellites. To lessen this vulnerability, the U.S. will need to invest in systems that enhance current military capabilities to monitor what is going on in space (space situational awareness), build new more responsive military space systems, and build defensive and offensive counter-space systems. Evidence also indicates that both the Chinese and the Russians are perfecting systems and plans for conducting cyber-warfare against the United States.[6] Despite the current trend lines of threat indicators, force planners must not fall into the trap expecting the next war to be similar to the previous, and plan based on those lessons learned by rebalancing defense capabilities too far in anyone direction.

Recommendation Three: Strategic Approach to Force Planning

An extended recession and an excessive national debt are clear signals the U.S. has reached culmination in its capacity to support the foreign policy and conflicts of the past decade. The U.S. requires a national security strategy and a force posture that is a reflection of the twenty-first century strategic environment and the nation's economic capacity to implement the strategy. The recently published Defense Strategic Guidance describes the projected security environment, key military missions, and capabilities for

---

[6] Peter Brookes, "The Cyberspy Threat: Foreign Hackers Target Military," *The New York Post*, April 29, 2009.

the Joint Force in 2020.[7] This document is intended to serve as a blueprint to guide decisions regarding the size and shape of the future force.[8]

This paper explored and highlighted a number of alternative approaches to force planning along with a thorough review of current and relevant strategic documents in order to formulate a recommended approach to force planning. The author compared each approach to the same evaluation criteria. The evaluation criteria are based on the ten primary missions listed in DoD's *Sustaining Global Leadership: Priorities for 21st Century* and the author's analysis on which approach by design is best suited to carry out a particular mission if the circumstance arises.

Evaluation Criteria
(Primary Mission of U.S Armed Forces as per DSG)

- Counter Terrorism and Irregular Warfare
- Deter and Defeat Aggression
- Project Power Despite Anti-Access/Area Denial Challenges
- Counter Weapons of Mass Destruction
- Operate Effectively in Cyberspace and Space
- Maintain a Safe, Secure, and Effective Nuclear Deterrent
- Defend the Homeland and Provide Support to Civil Authorities
- Provide a Stabilizing Presence
- Conduct Stability and Counterinsurgency Operations
- Conduct Humanitarian, Disaster Relief, and Other Operations

* IAW DSG: The aforementioned missions will largely determine the shape of the future Joint Force. The overall capacity of U.S. forces, however, will be based on requirements that the above subset of missions demand.

Figure 3. Evaluation Criteria[9]

---

[7] Department of Defense, *Sustaining Global Leadership: Priorities for 21st Century Defense*, January 2012, 1. http://www.defense.gov/news/defense_strategic_guidance.pdf (assessed May, 15, 2013).

[8] Ibid., 1.

Taking into account the current strategic environment and relevancy of the eight alternative approaches to force planning today (see table 2, pg.39), the author narrowed his focus to three approaches--Top Down, Hedging, Fiscal--that he determined to be the most adequate, feasible, and acceptable in his formulation of a recommended approach. (Figure 4, below).

Alternative Approaches to Force Planning

Top Down: National interest and objectives "drive" the top-down approach to force planning; it in turn, focuses principally on a nation's grand or national security strategy. The strengths of the top-down approach is first by helping strategist and force planners concentrate on ends. Second, it provides a systematic way to think through requirements from a broad, or "macro," perspective. Third, it emphasizes the relationship among the supporting instruments of national. There are certain pitfalls associated with this approach. First, it generally considers possible constraints only later in the planning process. Consequently, when dollar, technological, or other limits are applied, the distance between desires and constraints is often sufficiently great that major adjustments among the ends and means become necessary.

Hedging: The idea with this approach is to prepare fully for any conceivable tasking of military force. This technique seeks redundancy of systems, anticipates a wide range of employment options, and demands a balanced force that can deal with a wide range of contingencies from current problems to a very broad array of challenges often three or more decades into the future. The U.S. tends to hedge its force structure by providing for capabilities across the entire spectrum of the possible uses of military forces ranging from HADR, peacekeeping operations, and war against a potential near-peer power with nuclear forces. Its biggest fault is it can generate costly recommendations and requirements.

Fiscal: The fiscal approach is driven by budget and overall dollar constraints are fixed at the outset. Competing requirements within the government outside the military may also determine the fixed dollar amount in the military budget. A major weakness in this approach is the fiscal approach may not reflect changes in the international security environment, the nation's goals or its strategies. At worst, the fiscally driven approach may lead to unwise retention of a traditional "fair share" apportionment of funds rather than an integrated and rational allocation takes into account the changed security environment.

Figure 4. Designated Top Three Approaches to Force Planning[10]

---

[9] Author generated figure, source of data from, Department of Defense, *Sustaining Global Leadership: Priorities for 21st Century Defense*, January 2012, 4-6. http://www.defense.gov/news/defense_strategic_guidance.pdf (assessed May, 15, 2013).
[10] Author generated figure, source of data from, Naval War College (U.S.), *Strategy and Force Planning* (Newport, RI: Naval War College Press, 2000), 32.

In the comparison, the author evaluated all three force planning approaches against the established evaluation criteria and selected the force planning approach that best accomplished the mission (Figure 5, below). The values (1-5) reflect the relative advantages to mission accomplishment of each force planning approach. The ability to respond and the best likelihood of success in a particular mission area is rated with the highest numbers. All criteria have been weighted the same which means all ten primary mission areas are viewed as equally important in the force planning approach comparison.

Evaluation Criteria
(Primary Mission of U.S Armed Forces as per DSG)

Evaluation Criteria	Top-Down	Hedging	Fiscal
CT and IW	4	5	3
Deter and Defeat Aggression	5	5	3
Project Power Despite A2/AD	4	5	3
Counter WMD	5	5	3
Operate Effectively in Cyber & Space	5	5	3
Maintain Safe, Secure, & Effective Nuclear Deterrent	5	5	5
Defend the Homeland & DSCA	5	4	4
Provide a Stabilizing Presence	5	5	3
Conduct Stability & CI Ops	3	4	3
Conduct HADR & other Ops	4	4	2

Figure 5. Designated Top Three Approaches to Force Planning

Based on the author's evaluation criteria a hedging methodology that is fiscally informed is the recommended and best strategic approach to shaping the future force in an uncertain and fiscally constrained environment.

Hedging strategies are appropriate during times of strategic uncertainty. During the Cold War the adversary was known and the force could be structured accordingly, with well-understood qualitative and quantitative benchmarks. Currently, there are no existential threats to the U.S. that would garner a major mobilization of forces in the near or medium future.[11] Instead, the concern is that equipment acquired in large numbers today for such an improbable situation may draw funding and resources away from preparing for the type of operations that are much more likely. Worse, by the time a major conventional threat reappears--if it ever does--the equipment acquired may be obsolete given the rapid pace of technological change.[12]

Sequestration would likely require the United States to shed missions, commitments, and capabilities necessary to protect U.S. national security interests. The vital national interests of the U.S. have remained relatively constant; however, declining budgets will force the U.S. to prioritize the level interests in order to have the ability to pivot to the Asia-Pacific. The Pentagon has to be careful not to repeat past mistakes by reducing capabilities (such as ground forces) that provide a hedge against unexpected army/army-like threats. This is a recipe for high risk in an uncertain and dangerous world.

---

[11] John Mueller and Mark G. Stewart, "Hardly Existential," *Foreign Affairs*, April 2, 2010, http://www.foreignaffairs.com/articles/66186/john-mueller-and-mark-g-stewart/hardly-existential (assessed May 31, 2013)

[12] David W.Barno, Nora Bensahel, and Travis Sharp, "Pivot but Hedge: A Strategy for Pivoting to Asia while Hedging in the Middle East," *Orbis*, 2012, 163.

Today's much longer warning times allow hedging to be a practical option for managing the improbable threat of major conventional war while allowing scarce resources to be spent on forces appropriate for more immediate and pressing threats. The Pentagon's new strategic guidance presents a realistic way to maintain America's status as a global superpower in the context of shrinking defense dollars. But further cuts, especially at the level required by sequestration, would make this "pivot but hedge" strategy impossible to implement and would raise serious questions about whether the United States can continue to play the central role on the global stage. Finally, a hedging strategy is dynamic, not static, and requires constant monitoring of the strategic environment for changes.[13]

Recommendation Four: Fiscally Informed Force Modernization

As previously mentioned, DoD's *"Sustaining Global Leadership: Priorities for 21st Century Defense"* highlights ten primary mission areas the administration and defense leaders viewed as necessary for the Joint Force to recalibrate and invest in particular capabilities.[14] Given the uncertain strategic environment, the U.S. will have to maintain a broad portfolio of military capabilities that offer versatility across the range of required missions. As fiscal constraints are overlaid on a hedge approach in force structure and modernization, a smaller, lighter, more agile, and flexible joint force to conduct a full range of military activities will be all that is affordable to defend U.S. national interests. The U.S. political leadership has to makes it clear to the nation what are its national interests as DoD continues to review and adapt its priorities for the coming decade.

---

[13] Ibid., 173.
[14] Department of Defense, *Sustaining Global Leadership:*, 4-6.

The FY 2013 President's budget focuses investment funding on improving network operations, modernizing combat vehicles and aviation, and preserving a viable acquisition strategy.[15] All of these modernization investments are needed, but the Pentagon is not able to plan or budget for them adequately without a budget from Congress. A smaller joint force must employ both lessons from past and recent conflicts in order to avoid the pitfalls that led to the "hollow forces" of the past. DoD's approach to modernization must assess risk, set priorities, and make hard choices. The author recommends the DoD relook at its shipbuilding and aircraft modernization procurement programs to ensure the right mix of ships, aircraft and weapons platforms are appropriated for as the U.S. calls for a shift in focus to the Asia-Pacific region as number of ballistic missile defense ships have been reduced along with the purchase of fewer fifth generation fighters.[16] The Army has already skipped a generation of modernization in its combat vehicle fleet and is at increased risk each year of further delays.[17] Cyber security remains largely ignored and could become an even greater vulnerability in the future.[18]

---

[15] Julie Rudowski, "Fiscal Year 2013 Army Budget: Good-Bad-Ugly," Association of the United States Army, http://www.ausa.org/publications/ausanews/archives/2012/04/Pages/FiscalYear2013ArmybudgetGood-Bad-Ugly.aspx (assessed June 6, 2013).

[16] Jim Talent and Mackenzie Eaglen, "The Dangers of Defunding Defense," The Journal of International Security Affairs, http://www.securityaffairs.org/issues/2011/20/talent&eaglen.php (assessed June 6, 2013).

[17] "The Army has Already Skipped a Generation of Weapons," Association of the United States Army, www.ausa.org/publications/torchbearercampaign/.../issue2.pdf (assessed June 6, 2013)

[18] Jim Talent and Mackenzie Eaglen, "The Dangers of Defunding Defense," The Journal of International Security Affairs, http://www.securityaffairs.org/issues/2011/20/talent&eaglen.php (assessed June 6, 2013).

Conclusion

The U.S. faces profound challenges that require strong, agile, and capable military forces whose actions are harmonized with other elements of U.S. national power. The country's global responsibilities are significant and it cannot afford to fail. The balance between available resources and security needs has never been more delicate.

More than ever a budget that brings military and entitlement spending into balance is the desired means to achieve strategic ends. Since 1965 the U.S. government has been unable to balance military and domestic spending (Reagan build-up was an anomaly). Budget pressures have curtailed military spending since the end of the Cold War. What budget decisions must be made to build a force that can support a fiscally informed hedging strategy? Budget cuts and drawdowns may not be as significant as investment in force development. But, all this must be based on a clearly defined strategy.

President Eisenhower's balanced approach to domestic and foreign policy should serve as a model for the current and future administrations. He understood viability of hard and soft power depended on a strong economy. Eisenhower steered a balanced course economically. He helped strengthen established programs such as Social Security while pursuing a balanced approach, continuing most of the New Deal and Fair Deal programs, and emphasizing a balanced budget, unlike today where ever-increasing entitlement spending is putting pressure on key spending priorities, such as national defense, a core constitutional function of government.[19] Defense spending has declined

---

[19] Gerhard Peters and John T. Woolley, "Harry S. Truman, Annual Budget Message to the Congress: Fiscal Year 1950," The American Presidency Project, (assessed January 15, 2013). http://www.presidency.ucsb.edu/ws/?pid=13434

significantly as spending on the three major entitlements - Social Security, Medicare, and Medicaid - has more than tripled.[20] Eisenhower found the right combination of low taxes, balanced budgets, and public spending that allowed the economy to prosper.

It is key that President Obama and Congressional Leaders understand that current entitlement spending is unsustainable and is the key driver of future deficits. Rather than tackle them directly, some would recommend cutting defense. But even if spending on this crucial national priority was eliminated completely, entitlements would continue to drive deficits to unmanageable levels. Defense spending is also set to decrease in real terms over the long term. As such, the Pentagon will have to grapple with dwindling resources (a trend not seen in the past decade). This may be a serious challenge given the vectors of cost escalation that is expected.[21] Future military operations must be carried out as a part of a larger comprehensive, whole of government approach to problem solving. This also must include partner nations, government partner agencies, and the private non-governmental sector. The U.S. can ill afford to let history continue to repeat itself and from a national security perspective have a military force that is unable to deploy, fight and win our nation's wars and protect its interest.

---

[20] U.S. Office of Management and Budget, *Historical Tables, Budget of the United States Government, Fiscal Year 2012*, Febuary 14, 2011, 55.
[21] Anthony H. Cordesman and Robert Shelala, *The FY 2013 Defense Budget, Deficits, Cost-Escalation, and Sequestration*, Center For Strategic & International Studies, http://csis.org/publication/fy2013-defense-budget-deficits-cost-escalation-and-sequestration (assessed June 12, 2013).

BIBLIOGRAPHY

Abernathy, M. Glenn, Dilys M. Hill, and Phil Williams. *The Carter Years: The President and Policy Making.* New York: St. Martin's Press, 1984.

"The Army has Already Skipped a Generation of Weapons." *Association of the United States Army.* www.ausa.org/publications/torchbearercampaign/.../issue2.pdf (assessed June 6, 2013)

Atesoglu, H. Sonmez. Defense Spending and Aggregate Output in the United States. Defense and Peace Economics, 2009.

Austin, D. Andrew. and Levit, Mindy R. *Trends in Discretionary Spending,* Congressional Research Service Report for Congress, July 10, 2009.

Auten, Brian J. *Carter's Conversion The Hardening of American Defense Policy.* Columbia: University of Missouri Press, 2008. <http://site.ebrary.com/id/10364845>.

Baker, Peter. "Panetta's Pentagon, Without the Blank Check." *The New York Times.* October 23, 2011. http://www.nytimes.com/2011/10/24/us/at-pentagon-leon-panetta-charts-change-of-course.html?_r=2&ref=leonepanetta&

Barno, David W., Bensahel, Nora and Sharp, Travis. "Pivot but Hedge: A Strategy for Pivoting to Asia while Hedging in the Middle East." *Orbis* 56, no. 2 (2012): 158-76.

Barro, Roberto. "Government Spending in a Simple Model of Endogenous Growth," Journal of Political Economy Vol 98, No. 5, Part 2, October 1990 (Universityof Chicago Press), 121-123Bowie, Robert and Immerman, Richard. *Waging Peace: How Eisenhower Shaped an Enduring Cold War Strategy.* New York, 1998.

Brookes, Pete. "The Cyberspy Threat: Foreign Hackers Target Military," *The New York Post.* April 29, 2009. http://www.nypost.com/p/news/opinion/opedcolumnists/item_i0LdkztpHEzax71VdJdRmN;jsessionid=269EDF2FB2B038D2894C95693E4B8FF5

Bush, George, and Scowcroft, Brent. *A World Transformed.* New York, 1998.

Callahan, David. *Dangerous Capabilities: Paul Nitze and the Cold War.* New York, NY: HarperCollins, 1990.

Carpenter, Raymond W. "Army National Guard: Integrated Missions." Army 59, no. 10 (2009): 123-128. http://search.proquest.com.ezproxy6.ndu.edu/docview/237080797?accountid=12686.

Carter, Jimmy. "Budget Message to the Congress Transmitting the Fiscal Year 1981 Budget." (Washington, DC: The White House, January 28, 1980). http://www.presidency.ucsb.edu/ws/?pid=32851(accessed March 23, 2013).

Carter, Jimmy. *Keeping Faith: Memoirs of a President.* New York: Bantam, 1982.

Cheek, Michael." Mullen: National Debt is a Security Threat." *Executive Gov.* August 27, 2010. http://www.executivegov.com/2010/08/mullen-national-debt-is-a-security-threat/ (assessed May 31, 2013).

Clem, Harold J. *Mobilization Preparedness.* Washington, D.C.: National Defense University, 1983.

Clinton, William. "Remarks on Signing Emergency Supplemental Appropriations and Rescissions Legislation and an.." Weekly Compilation of Presidential Documents 31, no. 30 (07/31, 1995): 1309, http://ezproxy6.ndu.edu/login?url=http://search.ebscohost.com/login.aspx?direct=true&db=aph&AN=9509075379&site=ehost-live&scope=site.

Collender, Stanley E. and Urban Institute. *The Guide to the Federal Budget.* Washington, D.C.: Urban Institute Press, 1985.

Collins, J. Lawton. *War in Peacetime; the History and Lessons of Korea,.* Boston: Houghton Mifflin, 1969.

104th Congress. Section 923 of Public Law 104-201, *National Defense Authorization Act, 1997.* http://www.nps.gov/legal/laws/104th/104-201.pdf (accessed April 20, 2013).

Congressional Budget Office, *Long-Term Implications of the Fiscal Year 2010 Defense Budget.* January 2010.

Congressional Budget Office, *Total Qualities and Unit Procurement Cost Tables 1974-1995,* April 13, 1995, A8. http://www.cbo.gov/publication/18099 (assessed May 20, 2013).

Cook, James L. 2014. "2012 Defense Strategy Review &Amp; FY 2013 Defense Budget Request: Strategy &Amp; Fiscal Constraints". *Orbis.* 57, no. 1: 41-58.

Cordesman, Anthony H., and Burke Arleigh A. *The FY2013 Defense Budget, Sequestration, and Growing Strategy-Reality Gap.* Center for Strategic & International Studies, July 16, 2012.

Cordesman, Anthony H. and Shelala, Robert. *The FY 2013 Defense Budget, Deficits, Cost-Escalation, and Sequestration*, Center For Strategic & International Studies, http://csis.org/publication/fy2013-defense-budget-deficits-cost-escalation-and-sequestration (assessed June 12, 2013).

CSAF Strategic Studies Group. "What is a Hollow Force?" http://www.af.mil/shared/media/document/AFD-120213-053.pdf

Davidson, Phillip B. Vietnam at War : The History, 1946-1975. London: Sidgwick & Jackson, 1989.

Department of Defense, Sustaining Global Leadership: Priorities for 21st Century Defense, January 2012. http://www.defense.gov/news/defense_strategic_guidance.pdf

Donovan, Robert J. and Robert J. Donovan. *The Presidency of Harry S. Truman Tumultuous Years, 1949 - 1953*. New York, NY: Norton, 1982.

Dormandy, Xenia. "Prepared for Future Threats? US Defence Partnerships in Asia-Pacific Region." Chatham House, June 2012. http://www.chathamhouse.org/publications/papers/view/183803 (assessed April 25, 2013)

Durie, Eric. "Department of the Navy Response to Sequestration." Navy Live, March 2, 2013, http://navylive.dodlive.mil/2013/03/02/department-of-the-navy-response-to-sequestration/

Erdossy, Marty. "Why does the United States Only Have Eleven Aircraft Carriers?" *Forbes*. July 17, 2012. http://www.forbes.com/sites/quora/2012/07/17/why-does-the-united-states-only-have-eleven-aircraft-carriers/

Everstine, Brian and Weisgerber, Marcus. "Reduced Flying Hours Forces USAF To Ground 17 Combat Air Squadrons." Defense News. Apr. 8, 2013, http://www.defensenews.com/article/20130408/DEFREG02/304080011/Reduced-Flying-Hours-Forces-USAF-Ground-17-Combat-Air-Squadrons

Feickert, Andrew, Daggett, Stephen and Library of Congress. Congressional Research Service. "A Historical Perspective on "Hollow Forces." Congressional Research Service. (assessed January 15, 2012).

———. "A Historical Perspective on "Hollow Forces." Congressional Research Service.

Feickert, Andrew and Henning, Charles A. "Army Drawdown and Restructuring Background and Issues for Congress." Congressional Research Service.

Franklin, Daniel P. Making Ends Meet: Congressional Budgeting in the Age of Deficits. Washington, D.C. 1993.

Freedman, Lawrence. Kennedy's Wars: Berlin, Cuba, Laos, and Vietnam. New York: Oxford University Press, 2000.

Gaddis, John Lewis. *Strategies of Containment : A Critical Appraisal of American National Security Policy during the Cold War*. New York: Oxford University Press, 2005.

Gaddis, John Lewis. Cold War Statesmen Confront the Bomb: Nuclear Diplomacy since 1945. Oxford; New York: Oxford University Press, 1999.

Gaddis, John Lewis. *We now know: Rethinking Cold War History*. New York: Oxford University Press, 1997.

Gallup, "Most important problem." Gallup. http://www.gallup.com/poll/1675/most-important-problem.aspx. (assessed June 4, 2013).

Gates, Robert. "American Enterprise Institute (Defense Spending)."Office of Assistant Secretary of Defense (Public Affairs) Washington, D.C., May 24, 2011. http://www.defense.gov/speeches/speech.aspx?speechid=1570 (assessed March 22, 2013).

Gates, Robert "Hearing to Receive Testimony on the Challenges Facing the Department of Defense," January 27, 2009, http://www.armed-services.senate.gov/Transcripts/2009/01%20January/A%20Full%20Committee/09-02%20-%201-27-09.pdf (assessed May 15, 2013).

Gates, Robert. Remarks to the Greater Dallas Chamber of Commerce, May 3, 2007, http://www.defense.gov/transcripts/transcript.aspx?transcriptid=3956 (assessed May 23, 2013).

Gates, Robert. United States Military Academy Speech, West Point, NY. http://www.defense.gov/speeches/speech.aspx?speechid=1539 (assessed April 21, 2013)

Gilmore, Gerry J. "Military Needs New Strategy for Present, Future Threats, General Says," American Forces Press Service, Virginia Beach, VA, May 12, 2009, http://www.defense.gov/news/newsarticle.aspx?id=54308 (assessed April 22, 2013).

Gordon, Philip H. "The End of the Bush Revolution." Foreign Affairs 85, no. 4 (Jul. - Aug., 2006): 75-86, http://www.jstor.org/stable/20032042.

Harrison, Todd. Avoiding a DoD Bailout, Center for Strategic and Budgetary assessment, October 2009.

Horton, Scott. "Eisenhower on the Opportunity Cost of Defense." The Stream. http://harpers.org/blog/2007/11/eisenhower-on-the-opportunity-cost-of-defense-spending/ (accessed January/10, 2013).

House Budget Committee. Update on Costs of Desert Shield/Desert Storm: Hearing Before the Committee on the Budget. 102nd Cong., 1st Sess., May 15, 1991.

Ignatius, David. "Ike offers lessons for Obama's 2nd term." The Washington Post. January 10, 2013.

Ippolito, Dennis S. and Army War College (U.S.). Strategic Studies Institute. "Budget Policy, Deficits, and Defense a Fiscal Framework for Defense Planning." Strategic Studies Institute, U.S. Army War College.

Ippolito, Dennis S. and National Defense University. Institute for National Strategic Studies. Blunting the Sword : Budget Policy and the Future of Defense. Washington, DC: National Defense University : For sale by the Supt. of Docs., U.S. G.P.O., 1994.

Jones, Jeffrey M. Americans Divided in Views of U.S. Defense Spending, Gallup, February 21, 2013. http://www.gallup.com/poll/160682/americans-divided-views-defense-spending.aspx

Jones, L. R. and Jerry McCaffery. Budgeting, Financial Management, and Acquisition Reform in the U.S. Department of Defense. Charlotte, N.C.: IAP-Information Age Pub., 2008.

Kennedy, Paul. *The Rise and Fall of the Great Powers*. New York, Random House 1987.

Korb, L.J., Conley, L., and Rothman, A. "A Return to Responsibility." Center for American Progress, July 14, 2011, http://www.americanprogress.org/issues/security/report/2011/07/14/10016/a-return-to-responsibility/ (assessed January 15, 2013).

Krepinevich, Jr., Andrew F. National Security Strategy in an Era of Growing Challenges and Resource Constraints. Center for Strategic and Budgetary Assessments Perspective. June 2010.

Laird, Melvin R. "A Strong Start in a Difficult Decade: Defense Policy in the Nixon-Ford Years." International Security 10, no. 2 (Autumn, 1985): 5-26, http://www.jstor.org/stable/2538826.

Leffler, Melvyn P.,. A Preponderance of Power : National Security, the Truman Administration, and the Cold War. Stanford, Calif.: Stanford University Press, 1992.

Lewis, Kevin N. The Disciplind Gap and Other Reasons for Humility and Realism in Defense Planning, New Challenges for Defense Planning: Rethinking How Much is Enough (Santa Monica, Calif.: RAND Corporation, 1994.

Marshall, Tyrone C. "Dempsey Describes Future Force at Warfighting Conference." American Forces Press Service. May 16, 2012.

http://www.defense.gov/News/NewsArticle.aspx?ID=116362 (assessed March 15, 2013).

Matloff, Maurice, and United States. Department of the Army. American Military History. Washington: Office of the Chief of Military History, U.S. Army; [for sale by the Supt. of Docs., U.S. Govt. Print. Off.], 1973.

McLeary, Paul. "War Game Exposes Gaps for U.S. Army," Defense News, April 1, 2013. http://www.defensenews.com/article/20130331/DEFREG02/303310003/War-Game-Exposes-Gaps-U-S-Army (assessed April 25, 2013).

McCormick, David,. The Downsized Warrior : America's Army in Transition. New York: New York University Press, 1998.

McTague, J. "Steering Clear of the Cliff." Barron's. http://online.barrons.com/article/SB50001424053111904706204578004182169208520.html (accessed Feb 10, 2013).

Merica, Dan. "Obama's national security policy resembles Eisenhower's," CNN, March 3, 2013, http://www.cnn.com/2013/02/26/politics/obama-eisenhower

Metz, Steven. Revising the Two MTW Force Shaping Paradigm A "Strategic Alternatives Report" from the Strategic Studies Institute. Carlisle, PA: The Institute, 2001. http://www.strategicstudiesinstitute.army.mil/pdffiles/pub297.pdf

The Miller Center, "American Presidents." University of Virginia. http://millercenter.org/president/truman/essays/biography/5

Mitchell, David and Massoud, Tansa George. "Anatomy of Failure: Bush's Decision-Making Process and the Iraq War." Foreign Policy Analysis 5, no. 3 (2009): 265-86. http://onlinelibrary.wiley.com/doi/10.1111/j.1743-8594.2009.00093.x/pdf (assessed May 15, 2013).

Morgan, Iwan W. Eisenhower Versus "the Spenders": The Eisenhower Administration, the Democrats, and the Budget, 1953-60. New York: St. Martin's Press, 1990.

Mount Holyoke College. "President Eisenhower's Remarks at Governors' Conference." https://www.mtholyoke.edu/acad/intrel/pentagon/ps7.htm (assessed June 9, 2013

Mueller, John and Stewart, Mark G. "Hardly Existential." Foreign Affairs, April 2, 2010. http://www.foreignaffairs.com/articles/66186/john-mueller-and-mark-g-stewart/hardly-existential (assessed May 31, 2013).

Mullen, Mike. Transcript from "The Hill-Tribute to Troops," http://www.jcs.mil/speech.aspx?ID=1413

Mullen, Michael Cheek: National Debt is a Security Threat. Executive Gov. August 27, 2010.

Murdoch, C.A. Planning for a Deep Defense Drawdown--part I, Center for Strategic & International Studies, May 2012. Mullen, Michael Cheek: National Debt is a Security Threat, Executive Gov, August 27, 2010.

U.S. Department of Defense, Quadrennial Defense Review Report, Washington, DC, February 2010. www.csis.org/files/publication/120522_DD_Interim_Report.pdf. (assessed Febuary 23, 2013).

Nash, Philip. "Bear any Burden? John F. Kennedy and Nuclear Weapons." Sage Public Administration Abstracts 26, no. 3 (1999).

Naval War College (U.S.). Strategy and Force Planning. Newport, RI: Naval War College Press, 2000

Nye, Joseph S. "Redefining the National Interest." *Foreign Affairs*, Vol. 78, No. 4 (Jul. - Aug., 1999): 22-35, http://www.jstor.org/stable/20049361 (assessed June 4, 2013).

Obama, Barack. "Remarks by the President at AIPAC Policy Conference," AIPAC Policy Conference, Washington, D.C., March 04, 2012, http://www.whitehouse.gov/the-press-office/2012/03/04/remarks-president-aipac-policy-conference-0

Obama, Barack. National Security Strategy, Washington, D.C..: US Government Printing Office, May 2011.

Perry, Mark,. Four Stars. Boston: Houghton Mifflin, 1989.

Peters, Gerhard and Woolley, John T. "Harry S. Truman, Annual Budget Message to the Congress: Fiscal Year 1950." The American Presidency Project. (assessed January 15, 2013). http://www.presidency.ucsb.edu/ws/?pid=13434

Peters, Gerhard and Woolley, John T. "George Bush: Statement on Transmitting the Annual National Security Strategy Report." March 20, 1990," The American Presidency Project. http://www.presidency.ucsb.edu/ws/index.php?pid=18270&st=national+security (accessed February 5, 2013).

Peters, Gerhard and Woolley, John T. "William J. Clinton: Address Before a Joint Session of Congress on Administration Goals." The American Presidency Project. http://www.presidency.ucsb.edu/ws/index.php?pid=47232&st=defense&st1=#axz z1livuk65I (accessed March 15, 2013).

Peters, Gerhard and Woolley, John T. "George W. Bush, Statement on Senate Action on Federal Budget Legislation." The American Presidency Project. http://www.presidency.ucsb.edu/ws/?pid=45683. (assessed March 18, 2013).

Peters, Gerhard and Woolley, John T. "George W. Bush, Remarks at the Swearing-In Ceremony for Donald H. Rumsfeld as Secretary of Defense." The American Presidency Project. http://www.presidency.ucsb.edu/ws/index.php?pid=45725&st=defense&st1=#axz z1livuk65I (assessed March 18, 2013).

Peters, Gerhard and Woolley, John T. "George W. Bush, Address to the Nation Announcing Strikes Against Al Qaida Training Camps and Taliban Military Installations in Afghanistan." The American Presidency Project. http://www.presidency.ucsb.edu/ws/?pid=65088, (assessed March 20, 2013).

Pogue, Forrest C. George C. Marshall, Statesman, 1945-1959 / Forew. by Drew Middleton. New York [etc.]: Viking Penguin, 1987.

Reeves, Richard,. President Reagan : The Triumph of Imagination. New York: Simon & Schuster, 2005.

Rostker, Bernard. I Want You! the Evolution of the all-Volunteer Force. Santa Monica, CA: RAND, 2006.

Rudowski, Julie. "Fiscal Year 2013 Army Budget: Good-Bad-Ugly." Association of the United States Army. http://www.ausa.org/publications/ausanews/archives/2012/04/Pages/FiscalYear20 13ArmybudgetGood-Bad-Ugly.aspx (assessed June 6, 2013).

Samuels, Richard J. and Sage Publications, inc. "Encyclopedia of United States National Jungkun Seo "The Party Politics of "Guns Versus Butter" in Post-Vietnam America". Journal of American Studies. 45, no. -336. 2: 317Security." Sage Publications.

Sarkesian, Sam C. U.S. National Security: Policymakers, Processes, and Politics. Boulder: L. Rienner, 1989.

Seo, Jungkun. "The Party Politics of Guns Versus Butter in Post-Vietnam America." Journal of American Studies 45. no. 2: 317-336.

Shanker, Thom."Mapping Military Needs, Aided by a Big Projection," The New York Times, September 11, 2012. http://www.nytimes.com/2012/09/12/us/top-general-dempsey-maps-out-us-military-future.html?_r=0

Shortal, John H. 1998. "20th-Century Demobilization Lessons". Military Review. 78, no. 5: 64.

Slantchev, B. National Security Strategy: The Vietnam War, 1954-1975. University of California-San Diego: University of California-San Diego, 2009.

Smithsonian National Museum of American History. "Cold War," Behring Center. http://amhistory.si.edu/militaryhistory/printable/section.asp?id=11

Stewart, Richard W. and Center of Military History. American Military History, Volume II : The United States Army in a Global Era, 1917-2008. Washington, D.C.: Center of Military History, U.S. Army : For sale by the Supt. of Docs., U.S. G.P.O., 2010.

Stone, Andrea. Aging Airforce Tankers Fly on Leaky Wings and Prayer, AOL News, February 22, 2010. http://www.aolnews.com/2010/02/22/aging-air-force-tankers-fly-on-leaky-wings-and-prayers/ (assessed May 22, 2013).

Strategic Defense Initiative Organization (U.S.). "Report to the Congress on the Strategic Defense Initiative." Report to the Congress on the Strategic Defense Initiative. (1985).

Talent, Jim and Eaglen, Mackenzie. "The Dangers of Defunding Defense." The Journal of International Security Affairs. http://www.securityaffairs.org/issues/2011/20/talent&eaglen.php (assessed June 6, 2013).

Tiron, Roxana. "Joint Chiefs chairman reiterates security threat of high debt." *The Hill*, http://thehill.com/homenews/administration/105301-mullen-reiterates-threat-excessive-debt-poses-to-nation (assessed June 10, 2013).

Troxell, John F. and Army War College (U.S.). Strategic Studies Institute. Force Planning in an Era of Uncertainty: Two-MRCs as a Force Sizing Framework. Carlisle Barracks, Pa.: Strategic Studies Institute, U.S. Army War College, 1997.

Tyson, Ann Scott. "Gates Warns of Militarized Policy; Defense Secretary Stresses Civilian Aspects of U.S. Engagement," The Washington Post, July 16, 2008. (assesses May 29, 2013).

United States. Department of Defense. Base Closure and Realignment Report. April 1991: 167-170.

United States. Dept. of Defense. and Les Aspin. Report on the Bottom-Up Review. Washington, D.C.: U.S. Dept. of Defense, 1993.

U.S. Department of Defense. Department of Defense Budget Estimates 2012. http://comptroller.defense.gov/defbudget/fy2013/budget_justification/index.html. (accessed February 18, 2013).

U.S. Department of Defense, Quadrennial Defense Review Report, Washington, DC, February 2010.

U.S. Office of Management and Budget, Historical Tables, Budget of the United States Government, Fiscal Year 2012.

Wishon, Jennifer. Obama Proposes Leaner, Meaner Defense Machine, CBN News, January 06, 2012. http://www.cbn.com/cbnnews/us/2012/January/Obama-Outlines-Strategy-for-Leaner-US-Military-/ (assessed April 21, 2013).

The U.S. Joint Forces Command (USJFCOM), The 2010 Joint Operational Environment Briefing, Government Printing Office/electronic publication, Washington D.C., 2010. http://www.jfcom.mil/newslink/storyarchive/2010/JOE_2010_o.pdf

The War Room, "Good Cop, Bad Cop, Consistent US Interests." National Security Network. http://nsnetwork.org/good-cop-bad-cop-consistent-us-interests/ (assessed June 4, 2013).

Williams, Rudi. "Rumsfeld Responds to Questions During Town Hall Meeting," American Forces Press Service, Aug. 10, 2001. http://www.defense.gov/News/NewsArticle.aspx?ID=44787

Wishon, Jennifer. "Obama Proposes Leaner, Meaner Defense Machine." CBN News, January 06, 2012. http://www.cbn.com/cbnnews/us/2012/January/Obama-Outlines-Strategy-for-Leaner-US-Military-/

Witteried, Peter F. and ARMY WAR COLL CARLISLE BARRACKS PA. The Strategy of Flexible Response. Ft. Belvoir: Defense Technical Information Center, 1972.

Woolley, J. and Peters, G. "Harry S. Truman: "Annual Message to the Congress on the State of the Union.," January 4, 1950." The American Presidency Project. http://www.presidency.ucsb.edu/ws/index.php?pid=13567#izz1krXZK4H4 (accessed Febuary 18, 2013).

Yarger, Harry R. Strategy and the National Security Professional: Strategic Thinking and Strategy Formulation in the 21st Century. Westport, Conn. Praeger Security International, 2008.

VITA

CDR Williams is a native of Warner Robins, Georgia. He earned a Bachelor of Arts degree in Economics from The Fort Valley State University and earned his commission through Officer Candidate School in 1995. CDR Williams' education also includes a Master of Science in Management from Florida Institute of Technology and a Master of Arts degree in National Security and Strategic Studies from the United States Naval War College.

Most recently he was assigned to the UNITED STATES FLEET FORCES COMMAND's N3-Fleet Antiterrorism directorate as the Branch Head for Assessments where he was charged with conducting comprehensive antiterrorism program reviews to evaluate the effectiveness and adequacy of antiterrorism program implementation throughout the Fleet.

As a Surface Warfare Officer his at sea assignments includes tours onboard USS KLAKRING (FFG 42), USS GEORGE WASHINGTON (CVN 73), USS THACH (FFG 43), COMMANDER DESTROYER SQUADRON SIX and USS KEARSARGE (LHD 3). CDR Williams was also assigned to the staff of Commander Second Fleet in the Operational Net Assessment Directorate as the Joint Assessment Cell Planner and Battle Watch Captain in the Joint Operations Center.